BANISHING ANONYMITY

MIDDLE AND HIGH SCHOOL ADVISEMENT PROGRAMS

John M. Jenkins
Bonnie S. Daniel

EYE ON EDUCATION
6 DEPOT WAY WEST, SUITE 106
LARCHMONT, NY 10538
(914) 833–0551
(914) 833–0761 fax
www.eyeoneducation.com

Library of Congress Cataloging-in-Publication Data

Jenkins, John M.
    Banishing anonymity: middle and high school advisement programs / by John M. Jenkins and Bonnie S. Daniel.
        p.   cm.
    ISBN 1-883001-97-8
    1. Counseling in middle school education—United States. 2. Counseling in secondary education—United States. 3. Teacher participation in educational counseling—United States. I. Daniel, Bonnie S., 1941– II. Title.

LB1620.5   J46 2000

                                 99-088802

10 9 8 7 6 5 4 3 2 1

Cover design by Carolyn H. Edlund
Editorial and production services provided by
Richard H. Adin Freelance Editorial Services
52 Oakwood Blvd., Poughkeepsie, NY 12603-4112
(914-471-3566)

Also Available from EYE ON EDUCATION

Personalized Instruction:
Changing Classroom Practice
by James Keefe and John Jenkins

Instruction and the Learning Environment
by James Keefe and John Jenkins

Motivating and Inspiring Teachers
by Todd Whitaker

What School Should Do to
Help Kids Stop Smoking
by William Fibkins

The Directory of Programs
for Students at Risk
by Thomas L. Williams

Making Decisions about Diverse Learners:
A Guide for Educators
by Fern Aefsky

Educating Homeless Students:
Promising Practices
Edited by James Stronge and Evelyn Reed-Victor

Dealing with Difficult Teachers
by Todd Whitaker

Delegation and Empowerment:
Working with and Through Others
by Michael Ward and Bettye MacPhail-Wilcox

Human Resources Administration:
A School-based Perspective
by Richard E. Smith

ABOUT THE AUTHORS

John M. "Jack" Jenkins has written over 50 articles and book chapters, co-edited 4 books, written 1 book, and co-authored 4 others. He is a former high school principal, as well as a former director of the P.K. Yonge Developmental Research School on the campus of the University of Florida. He is currently an educational consultant and adjunct professor in the College of Education, University of Florida, Gainesville. He also serves as the instruction department chair for the *International Journal of Educational Reform*. He was a member of the Carnegie/NASSP Commission on the Restructuring of the American High School that produced the report *Breaking Ranks*.

Bonnie S. Daniel is a former middle and high school English teacher, high school principal, team leader, curriculum writer, staff developer, English supervisor, and adviser to high school students. She had the privilege of working at a high school, now almost 30 years old, which made student advisement a priority since its inception. She presently teaches aspiring teachers and administrators at Towson University in Maryland.

ACKNOWLEDGMENTS

This book is the result of many years of practical applications of advocacy. Initially we were introduced to the concept of advisement as part of the National Association of Secondary Schools Model Schools Project (1969–1974). Advisement was a key component of the Model Schools Project. Each professional was expected to work closely with a finite number of students in an advisement capacity. As principal and as a teacher at Wilde Lake High School, Columbia, Maryland, we were directly involved with the implementation and practice of advisement.

In 1984, the Florida Legislature passed the Teachers-As-Advisors bill that offered the opportunity for middle and high schools in Florida to apply for grants to implement advisement. The late Senator Curtis Peterson, then President of the Florida Senate, was the guiding light behind the Florida program. Five years of funding from the Florida Legislature enabled over 200 middle schools and high schools to experiment with advisement programs. Dr. Jenkins served as a special consultant to the Florida State Department of Education working with schools and conducting an evaluation each of the 5 years.

The exemplary programs described in Chapter 2 were discovered as part of the Dr. Jenkins' work with the Florida State Department of Education and our work with the Model Schools Project. We are indebted to the contact persons in each of the schools for supplying us with complete information about their programs. Their help was invaluable in capturing the spirit of advisement resident in the schools.

We also acknowledge the teachers at Wilde Lake High School, many who served as advisers for over 25 years. Their willingness to implement innovative programs was instrumental in the success of advisement at one high school. Wilde Lake was one of the 34 schools in the Model Schools Project. As the school ends its 28th year, advisement is still a critical component of the school's organization. An article in *USA Today* (June 1, 1998) on the Class of 2000 closed with the following paragraph:

> The school (Wilde Lake High School) tries to help kids cope with problems, providing one adviser who stays with them throughout high school. The advisers give the teens one more adult to help deal with a difficult truth that permeates suburbs as well as inner cities. Life is a contact sport. Nobody comes away without scars.

TABLE OF CONTENTS

FOREWORD

There is no doubt in my mind that we cannot have a quality school without much more teacher/student involvement than is possible in an ordinary school. Having worked for years with Jack Jenkins, and having been associated with the kind of program at Wilde Lake High School, the kind of teacher/student advisement program that was used there is ideal to get students to begin to think that what they learn in school is adding quality to their lives. In a quality school, the students must be more than pupils. They must be our friends, and people with whom we talk on a continuing basis, not just when they are having difficulties. It is an ongoing dialogue so that every student feels involved with at least one person and that person is the key to the student's involvement in school and education. I strongly support what Dr. Jenkins and Ms. Daniel present in this book.

William Glasser, MD
Author, *Choice Theory:*
A New Psychology of
Personal Freedom (1998)

INTRODUCTION

THE CURRENT CONTEXT

In the wake of the Bay of Pigs invasion in April 1961, President John F. Kennedy quoted the infamous Italian fascist leader, Galeazzo Ciano, "Victory has a hundred fathers but defeat is an orphan." Applying this quote to schooling, those students who are successful in academics, athletics, or student activities have no trouble finding advocates. In fact, many of them have several adults who are willing to give them guidance or advice.

School practices such as awards assemblies and honor rolls are designed to give recognition to student accomplishments. Unfortunately, the other side of that coin is that students who fail to get recognized in one of these venues are not stimulated to do better. Rather, they often resent the students who get the rewards.

Annual school report cards show an uncomfortable increase in the number of students referred to an administrator for disciplinary action, in the number of students suspended from school both externally and internally and in the number of students choosing to leave school prior to graduation. The 28th Annual Phi Delta Kappan *Poll of the Public's Attitudes Toward the Public Schools* shows that drug abuse and lack of discipline are the most frequently mentioned problems facing the local public schools. Yet, goals adopted by the nation's governors in 1991, and emphasized at the national level by President Clinton, call for an increase in the graduation rate to 90 percent and the elimination of drugs, firearms, violence, and alcohol use on school campuses.

The Goals 2000 initiative also commits schools and school districts to achieving academic success for all students.

> All students will leave grades 4, 8, and 12 having demonstrated competency in challenging subject matter including English, mathematics, science, foreign languages, civics and government economics,

arts, history, and geography, and every school in America will ensure that all students learn to use their minds well so that they may be prepared for responsible citizenship.

The essence of this goal asks all schools to do something they have never done. It also raises the bar with regard to graduation rate because it is presumed if all students are competent in challenging subject matter and learning to use their minds well, they will choose to remain in school and graduate. Thus, the 90 percent statistic is transformed into 100 percent. More importantly, it places the future of a sizable number of students in serious jeopardy. When specific benchmarks for student achievement are adopted, the responsibility for helping individual students reach those plateaus falls to someone. Historically, the track record for schools has been to shift the burden to individual students and their parents. The rhetoric of school reform, however, seems to be saying that the schools must change.

BASIC NEEDS AND THEIR SATISFACTION

Psychiatrist William Glasser believes that all human beings are genetically required to satisfy the basic needs of survival, belonging, power, fun, and freedom. It is his contention that 100,000 genes are in a fertilized egg. Fifty thousand are contributed by the male and 50,000 by the female. Of the 100,000 total genes only 10,000 are required to create a human being. The other 90,000 migrate to the frontal lobe of the brain and create the five basic needs. In this way, all humans are similar. They differ in the ways in which they have learned to satisfy each need. In his book *Control Theory in the Classroom* (1986), Glasser states that to the degree these basic needs are adequately met, people become good citizens and productive workers.

Survival needs relate to air, food, water, shelter, and safety. For readers who are familiar with Maslow's hierarchy of needs, Glasser's survival needs are the first two steps of the hierarchy. He speculates that the survival needs may have come first and the other four needs were derived from them. By now, however, the other needs have become separate and stand alone.

Belonging needs refer to feeling a part of a family, a friendly group, a team, or an organization. Love, friendship, and a need for affiliation are all part of the need for belonging.

Power is tied to achievement and the recognition that comes with it. The need for power is also satisfied when people listen to what people have to say and act positively upon it.

Freedom is the need which relates to making decisions and having a say about what is done in an institution or organization. Giving people choices is a way to respond to their need for freedom.

Fun is the genetic reward for learning something new. It provides an internal incentive to learn. Individuals seem to have the most fun when they learn something that is need satisfying. Ostensibly, more money is spent in search of fun than any of the other basic needs.

When these needs are satisfied by a person, an experience or an institution, pictures representing those entities are placed in an individual's head. These images then constitute descriptions of how that individual wants the world to be. Students from poor socioeconomic conditions frequently have fewer positive options to satisfy their needs than do students from more affluent home environments. Yet, students representing all socioeconomic strata begin their school careers viewing school as a highly positive place. It is only after some students continue to fail in school and lose the support of significant adults that they remove the picture of school as a need satisfier.

A powerful remedy for this situation is the identification of a significant adult in the school environment who can work with students in an endeavor to reverse the cycle of failure where it exists and to support them in their quest to become more responsible people. Responsibility in this sense is defined as helping students to meet their basic needs in a manner that does not infringe upon other students meeting theirs. Unfortunately, many needy students look for support from their peers who often suffer the same debilitating effects of school failure and an inadequate home environment. What can schools do to expand their role in providing a significant adult for all students?

One approach with historical success is to assign each school professional a finite number of students to guide through their stay at a particular school. Such programs have their origin in public secondary schools since the beginning of the twentieth century, and in private schools since their inception. The idea that each student benefits from a close relationship with a significant adult seems almost tautological. The practice of providing such a service for all students has been nonexistent in many schools and often inadequately implemented in others. This book describes programs of advisement that work and offers specific ideas to initiate or improve such programs.

The book is addressed to principals, administrators, counselors, teachers, and parents who have an interest in improving the quality of their schools by giving *all* students the kind of support and care that is their inalienable right.

Chapter 1 explores the concept of advocacy and describes several historical precedents of achieving advocacy through advisement programs. It also explains how advisement is interwoven into a team approach for student welfare. Chapter 2 describes the setting for advisement and presents other school structures for knowing students well. Chapter 3 looks at several contemporary implementations of advisement programs at the middle and high school levels. Chapter 4 details how advisement programs are organized and describes the relationship of advisement to school guidance and counseling. Chapter 5 establishes expectations for advisers and clarifies the specific tasks that advisers do. Chapter 6 explores the kinds of staff development experiences advisers need in order to meet their responsibilities. Such things as choice theory and being able to interpret learning style differences in advisees are explored in depth. Chapter 7 helps school-based educators begin an advisement program. It offers a developmental approach to implementation allowing schools to start slowly and move at their own pace toward more sophistication. Chapter 8 reports findings in the literature that supports advisement programs and provides practical steps for gathering data from which to make program changes. It applies the concepts of formative and summative evaluation for determining school success in establishing and conducting an advisement program. The final chapter, Chapter 9, takes a longer view of advisement programs and examines its impact on the total culture of the school. Advisement and advocacy go hand-in-hand in making a school a better place for students and teachers.

The term advocacy means to support, to plead the cause of another. Among its synonyms are ally, defender, patron, promoter, and supporter. Interestingly, advocacy appears on the same page and in the same column in *Webster's New Collegiate Dictionary* as advise and advisement. Perhaps it is no coincidence that the words advisory and advocacy are next to each other in order. In *Personalized Instruction* (Eye On Education, 2000), Keefe and Jenkins include advisement as one of the key elements of personalized instruction. They see personalized instruction as the direction schools must take for the new century. In addition to advisement and coaching, personalized learning includes:

- Profiling learner characteristics;
- Creating a culture of collegiality characterized by a constructivist culture;
- Staff/student collaboration and cooperative social relations;
- An interactive learning environment;
- Flexible student scheduling and pacing; and
- Performance-based assessment.

These seven elements work together to enable schools to become places where all students retain knowledge, understand knowledge and apply knowledge toward the solution of real-world problems. Quality schooling is within reach of all students and educators.

We hope as a result of this book and educators who are willing to take risks, schools will become places where…

- All students feel they belong.
- No student loses interest because no one cares.
- Individual student progress is the number one priority.
- All students are accepted for who they are.
- Someone listens when students talk.

- Changes are made to accommodate student needs.
- All students are pushed to do better.
- Parents are involved and see school positively.
- No student is overlooked.

The new century is upon us. Schools can no longer be satisfied with continuing a status quo where some students are regarded as more important than others. Schools are replete with practices that divide rather than unite student bodies. Success for all students is not a tacit form of social promotion. It is a wish for students to keep school in their quality worlds, and in this regard, one person can make a difference. Advocacy and advisement are two ways of saying the same thing. Support for all students is a basic need! Join us in a quest to fashion a school environment that says yes to all students and helps them take effective control of their lives.

Jack Jenkins
Bonnie Daniel

1

WHO ARE THE ADVOCATES?

Advocates for students can be found in all schools. For some students it is a teacher to whom they can easily relate. For others it is a coach, a music director, or an activity sponsor. The advocates are school personnel who find time to help individual students with their academic or personal problems. Coaches frequently become advocates for student athletes because the time spent in team activities fosters development of a special athlete-coach relationship. In times of crisis or special need, student athletes naturally gravitate toward their coaches. Band and choral directors often establish similar relationships with their students. Classroom teachers who have devoted extra time to certain students can become their advocates. Every school-based educator knows of situations where students have developed trust and special regard for a coach, music director or teacher. It is apparent that the teaching methods of these faculty members encourage formation of close student-teacher relationships. Unfortunately, due to the high student:teacher ratio at most schools, it is logistically impossible for faculty members to develop special relationships with all of the students they teach or coach.

At first glance, it appears that guidance counselors are in the best position to serve as advocates for students. However, the typical public high school has a counselor:counselee ratio of more than 300:1, which demonstrates why a guidance counselor cannot establish a meaningful relationship with each student. In fact, most counselors meet with most of their counselees only once during each school year. Only the small number of students who seek scholarships or have academic difficulties actu-

1

ally see counselors more frequently. Because of the arbitrary nature of counselor assignments, their duties are often limited to assisting in course registration, disseminating college and career information, and facilitating schedule changes. Yet, students need a buffer who they can trust to give them sound advice and answer their questions and resolve their problems.

EXPANDING ADVOCACY
THROUGH ADVISEMENT

A school can combat the anonymity that frequently accompanies high student:teacher, student:guidance counselor, or student:administrator ratios by designating a specific teacher or administrator as the person responsible for monitoring the academic progress of a manageable number of students. In this way, students would know they could always request assistance from their designated teacher-advisers. By working with each of their assigned students on an individual basis, teacher-advisers become very well-acquainted with their individual advisees. If an advisee has a school problem, the designated teacher-adviser can consult with another teacher or administrator and provide information about an individual student's interests, aspirations and activities.

The benefits of an advisement program can be seen from evaluations conducted over a 5-year period in 122 high schools and 135 middle schools in Florida. Sixty percent of the high schools showed a decrease in the number of students who chose to leave school prior to graduation. One Miami high school reported a decrease in dropouts from 11.5 percent to 4.7 percent over a two-year period and one rural school noted a 7.46 percent reduction in one year (Jenkins, 1992).

For the schools that participated in the study, implementation of an advisement program was uniformly followed by an increase in parent participation. Data collected from these parents showed that they willingly participated in conferences at which they discussed course planning, academic progress and out-of-school interests with their children's advisers. At one school with a plethora of migrant students, parents met with advisers on report card days to discuss their children's progress.

All of the parents attended the conferences held on each of the six report card days (Jenkins, 1992).

Improvements in school attendance were observed in over half the participating schools in 1990. Advisers frequently called the homes of absent advisees to inquire about health and to offer help in getting school assignments. In some cases, they called after each absence. In other cases, the advisers telephoned advisees homes after their third to fifth absence. The advisers viewed improvement in attendance as an important aspect of their responsibilities for helping their advisees improve academically. Because since school attendance seems closely aligned with school achievement, gains in student grade point averages were attributed to an increase in time spent at school. Interestingly, there seems to be a direct correlation between the duration of a school's involvement in the advisement program, and:

- Reduction of its dropout rate;
- Increase in parental participation; and
- Improvement in daily attendance (Jenkins, 1992).

Teacher-advisers become well-acquainted with their advisees by working with them on a continuous basis over the course of several years. The teacher-adviser can use information gleaned from these relationships to tailor curriculum and instruction to create an appropriate educational plan for each individual student (Jenkins, 1998).

Historically, the earliest reference to the idea of advisement at the secondary level can be found in the Dalton Laboratory Plan, which was developed by Helen Parkhurst in 1921 at the high school in Dalton, Massachussetts. The Dalton Plan replaced traditional classrooms with laboratory settings for specific subject areas. Students worked in the laboratories on educational contracts under the direction of one or more teachers. The students met each morning with their homeroom teachers to choose the contracts on which they wished to work and the time to be spent in the appropriate laboratory setting (Edwards, 1991).

Although there was no mention of the term "adviser" in the Dalton Plan, the functions of the homeroom teachers were very similar to the responsibilities assumed by teacher-advisers. The original role of the homeroom teacher in the American secondary schools seemed closely aligned with advisement. The homeroom concept was one of a home base for each student. Homeroom teachers were expected to know more about their homeroom students than they were about the students in their regular classes. Graduate courses entitled "Guidance for the Classroom Teacher" were often instituted to prepare teachers for the additional responsibilities of the homeroom.

The first formal advisement program was found at the New Trier High School in Winnetka, Illinois in 1924. This "Adviser-Personnel Plan," as it was called, was "...designed to provide educational, vocational, social, moral, and ethical guidance and counsel to all the students in the school" (Clerk, 1928, p. 1). At New Trier, teacher-advisers were assigned by grade levels and remained with their advisees throughout their high school careers. An adviser chairperson, usually a teacher, was assigned to oversee a group of advisers. The adviser chairpersons reported directly to the Deans of Students who served as the executive heads of the adviser system.

The advisers were expected to serve as both teachers and friends to their advisees. Advisers were expected to visit the homes of their advisees prior to Thanksgiving of each school year. The personal nature of the New Trier System is captured in the following description in the Adviser-Personnel Plan: "The adviser is expected to study each one of the advisees with the greatest care and sympathy with a view to understanding him thoroughly and gaining his confidence" (Clerk, 1928, p. 13). When a New Trier teacher believed discipline of a student was necessary, the matter was referred to the student's adviser, who was specifically directed to not punish the advisee. Instead, the adviser was instructed to discuss the subject of the referral with the advisee, and to then endeavor to resolve the difficulty. An adviser was required to inform the referring teacher of the disposition of a disciplinary referral.

Under the New Trier System, advisers were required to be in their classrooms by 8:15 AM in order that individual conferences could be scheduled for after school hours. Also, an adviser period was scheduled each day from 8:30 AM to 9:00 AM. Mandatory, grade-level specific material to be covered during this period was specified for two days of each week. For the other three days of the week, advisers were free to create their own lesson plans for this period, provided that the teacher focused on either individual counseling or group activities.

In 1956, additional goals for advisement were stated. Advisory groupings were designed to combat the increased size of the New Trier High School student body. The advisory groupings were intended to provide students with a "home away from home." Advisers were given the responsibility of identifying students with serious emotional problems and referring those students to professional counselors. .

Two years later, the New Trier Parent Association completed a list of objectives this association considered important to the adviser system. The number one priority was to provide an opportunity for the students, within the context of the large school environment, to develop the types of relationships characteristic of a small community. The New Trier Parent Association also emphasized the importance of the adviser as the liaison between home and school. Based on the results of a study conducted by the North Central Association of Colleges and Schools, the *1970-71 New Trier Student Guide Book* stressed that the adviser was intended to be a personal counselor for students, providing assistance which would help students to live intellectually, emotionally, socially, and morally fulfilling lives.

The Model Schools Project, sponsored by the National Association of Secondary School Principals and the Danforth Foundation (1969-74), proposed the notion of teacher-adviser as a key ingredient in reforming secondary education. Advisement was one of several innovations that schools participating in the Project were expected to implement. In addition to advisement, model schools implemented:

- ♦ A continuous progress system of curriculum and instruction;
- ♦ A new approach to grading;
- ♦ A differentiated staffing pattern;
- ♦ The liberal use of the community for learning;

- A flexible schedule that matched time with the tasks to be accomplished;
- Three different but supportive approaches to instruction (large group, small group, and independent study); and
- A redefinition of curriculum into essential learnings, desirable learnings and quest.

Dr. J. Lloyd Trump, director of the Model Schools Project and Director of Research for NASSP, reasoned that implementing "all at once" change was more efficacious to the success of each of the elements than if schools were to implement one new idea at a time.

Teacher-advisers were crucial to the success of a personalized education process that included diagnosis, prescription, implementation, and evaluation. By knowing each of their advisees as "a total human being educationally," (a phrase coined by Dr. Trump), teacher-advisers helped their advisees with educational decisions and personal difficulties and monitored their academic progress closely. Teacher-advisers were viewed as the first line of defense when an advisee experienced difficulty. In some of the advanced model schools, advisers were empowered to schedule advisees in learning environments for a mutually agreed-upon length of time. If an advisee wanted to work a half day or a whole day on a science project, the adviser was empowered to make that decision. Advisers could change advisees' schedules on a daily and weekly basis. The proximity of the adviser and the advisee created a friendly, mutually respectful bond that resulted in each student having at least one adult advocate in the school.

In schools participating in the Model Schools Project, advisers met with their advisees each day, sometimes in advisory group meetings similar to the New Trier model and sometimes with individual students, simply to validate an advisee's schedule for a given day. Each participating public school designated eight subject areas for large group instruction, while the participating Roman Catholic schools added religion to the list and hence designated nine large group instruction subjects. This list of large group instruction subjects was not alterable by the adviser, nor were the follow-up small group discussions where students could clarify points presented in the large group. Group meetings of band, orchestra, and chorus were also inalterable. Everything else, however, was between the adviser and the individual advisee.

It was the teacher-adviser in the Model Schools Project who literally determined the success of the total project. Without the adviser system as part of the total change plan, students could get lost or simply make little or no academic progress. Ostensibly, this is the main reason that nonparticipating schools adopted the advisement component of the Model Schools Project more readily than the Project's other innovations. Unfortunately, in schools that adopted only the Project's advisement component, there were problems when teachers' schedules were too inflexible to give them adequate time to be effective advisers. During the Model Schools Project, it was estimated that teachers required five hours a week to devote exclusively to advisement if the program were to be successful. Consequently, flexible schedules for teachers were as much a requirement as flexible schedules for students. One could not expect a teacher to teach five classes per day and then be an adviser in addition. Instead, time for advisement had to be built into a teacher's schedule.

Because the Model Schools Project advocated a differentiated staff, the participating schools were advised to trade teaching positions for various teacher-aide positions. When this was done, it increased the teacher-student ratio but decreased the student-adult ratio in a school. With fewer teachers to assign as advisers it was not unusual to have 30 to 35 advisees assigned to one teacher-adviser. This was the case even in schools where the principal, assistant principals, and professional staff also served as advisers. When a large number of advisees was assigned to a teacher-adviser, it was often logistically impossible to build a personal rapport between the advisee and the adviser. This condition was tempered by the requirement that advisers conduct nine or ten individual conferences with each advisee during each school year.

Guidance was considered part of the curriculum. As in other subject areas, a scope and sequence was developed by the guidance staff. The content of the curriculum was delivered by teacher-advisers and by professional counselors. It included areas such as school orientation, academic alternatives, vocational options, available pupil personnel services, test interpretation and criteria for college selection. Just as reading, writing and mathematics were considered basic skills so was information about getting a job, entering college, preparing credentials, taking and interpreting tests and selecting the tests to take in the first place.

In January 1990, the Carnegie Council on Adolescent Development published *Turning Points: Preparing Youth for the 21st Century*, a report of its Developmental Task Force on Education for Young Adolescents. The report was directed at the reform of middle level education in the United States. The Task Force reasoned that "many middle schools now fall far short of meeting the educational, health and social needs of millions of young adolescents" and that "many youth now leave the middle grades unprepared for what lies ahead of them" (Carnegie Council on Adolescent Development, 1990, p. 10). They saw the impersonal nature of large schools as a major obstacle to creating the kind of community of learning that nurtures individual student achievement. The initial cluster of recommendations focused on the need to create a climate for learning in each middle school. Among the three specific recommendations in this section was the following:

> Assign an adult adviser for every student. Every student should be well known by at least one adult in the middle grade school. Currently, guidance counselors in middle grade schools may be responsible for 500 students or more. Such caseloads spread the talents and training of guidance counselors impossibly thin. Through small-group advisories, homerooms, or other arrangements, teachers and other staff can become mentors to and advocates for students, as well as the primary contact for parents. Advisers should remain with the students throughout their middle grade experience. Guidance counselors would retain critical functions in supervising teachers in their advisory role and counseling students

with problems that go beyond advisor training. (Carnegie Council on Adolescent Development, 1990, p. 12).

The Carnegie Council Task Force report clearly differentiated the role of the teacher-adviser from that of the professional counselor. The role of the adviser was one of academic advisement, parent contact, and advocacy. They were not to step outside the limits of their training and attempt to solve personal problems. These problems were the purview of the professional counselor. This distinction echoed the message of the Model Schools Project. Teacher-advisers were to provide help to advisees only in their areas of competence. They were to avoid assuming the role of surrogate psychologist.

The unabridged version of the Carnegie Council Task Force report cited the advisement program at the Shoreham-Wading River Middle School, Shoreham, New York, as an exemplar of a middle grades advisement program. Their advisory system was described as the "core organizing principle of the school" (Maeroff, 1990, p. 506). In addition, the Carnegie Council Task Force report highlighted aspects of the Shoreham advisory program that included advisement activities of 72 minutes per day in the daily schedule. Students met with their advisers each day in a variety of settings from one-on-one conferences to eating lunch with them to going on excursions in the community. Advisement was described as the number one priority in personalizing the educational program.

In 1994, the National Association of Secondary School Principals and the Carnegie Foundation for the Advancement of Teaching jointly sponsored a commission to investigate the needs for high school education in the new century. The commission's report, *Breaking Ranks: Changing an American Institution,* contained 82 recommendations to improve high school education. Under the chapter heading "The School Environment, Creating a Climate Conducive to Teaching and Learning" were seven recommendations, the third of which states, "Every high school student will have a Personal Adult Advocate to help him or her personalize the educational experience."

The text elaborating this recommendation began as follows: "Each student needs to know that at least one adult in the school is closely concerned with his or her fate. The Personal Adult Advocate is that person" (National Association of Secondary School Principals, 1996, p. 31). The narrative elaborating this recommendation described the advocate's role as broader than that of the typical homeroom teacher. The joint commission's report envisioned that advocates' relationships with their high school students would be far more significant than the relationships which emerge from daily contact with teachers and coaches. The joint commission's report mandated that the personal adult advocates become so well acquainted with individual students that the advocates could help the students to develop "personal plans for progress" to guide them through high school. Additionally, to facilitate the student's dealings with others in the school, the report required regular meetings between advocates and each of their 15 to 20 student-advisees. (National Association of Secondary School Principals, 1996)

While the term adviser is never mentioned in this recommendation or any other recommendation, the parallel between the adviser role and the advocate role is easily seen. Actually, they appear to be one and the same. The idea undergirding advisement or advocacy is that every student has an inalienable right to a successful school experience. Placing an adult advocate in close proximity with each student increases the likelihood that salient information about the student can be collected and used to develop an individualized education plan.

Personalizing the process of education implies that information about each student will be gathered systematically and disseminated to teachers who have a vested interest in the student. Advisers play a key role in gathering and interpreting information about advisees and in helping them to use that information to develop an appropriate learning plan for their high school careers and beyond.

THE GUIDANCE TEAM APPROACH: FOCUS ON STUDENT WELFARE

Advisement is part of a total school guidance program. It differs from the work of the professional counselor in that the adviser rarely has the formal education to provide a sophisticated level of personal and academic counseling. The existence of teacher-advisers in the school enables professional counselors to work with more serious student problems. By working cooperatively, advisers and counselors can offer appropriate services for all students in a school.

Keefe (1983) sees guidance activities as quasi-administrative or clinical depending on the purpose. He defines the major guidance services as:

- *Career Information.* Vocational and college materials made available in special centers, through resource persons, college nights and career days.

- *Instructional Units.* Teaching units focusing on orientation, career/college planning and student concerns.

- *Registration and Placement.* Registering students for the next year or term, assisting in class assignment, providing college/job recommendations, and employment referrals.

- *Records Maintenance.* Establishing personal counseling files on each student.

- *Testing.* Administering and supervising individual and group tests, including standardized, criterion-referenced and competency examinations.

- *Counseling.* Personalized, one-to-one contact for planning, problem solving or placement.

- *Referral.* Therapeutic referral to district psychologists and specialists, community agencies and outside professions.

In regard to advisement, Keefe (1983) said that advisement focuses on the instructional end of the guidance continuum. It cuts across several of the guidance functions that do not require specialized training.

Figure 1.1 provides a brief explanation and tidy summation of the relationships among the components of the list, above. Taken together, the definition list and its diagrammatical representation constitute Keefe's guidance continuum.

FIGURE 1.1. AN OVERVIEW OF A SCHOOL
GUIDANCE PROGRAM (KEEFE, 1983, P. 3)

Career Informa- tion	Guidance Units	Registra- tion & Place- ment	Records Mainte- nance	Testing	Coun- seling	Referral

Advisement

Instructional   Therapeutic

Professional counselors work directly with teacher-advisers and with students referred to them by advisers. The usual counselor:advisers ratio is between 1:12 and 1:15 This arrangement allows the counselor to plan and execute staff development activities for advisers, meet with individual advisers regularly, and arrange for referrals of individual students to services beyond the school. It also frees the counselors to work with teachers and students to achieve more complete personalization of instruction throughout the school. This aspect of counseling has been one of the most neglected in recent school history. Professional counselors, by nature of their training, are in a position to help teachers and advisers to develop individual learning plans for each student.

For example, in the past 10 to 15 years the concept of learning style has become prominent as a means to tailor instruction to the individual needs of students. Learning style instruments abound. Helping teachers and advisers select an appropriate instrument, administer it, and interpret the results can advance the cause of personalized learning throughout a school. Counselors can also help teachers create appropriate ways to determine the success of style-based instruction.

Advisers, working with smaller numbers of advisees than the typical counselor:counselee ratio, are able to assume responsibility for a number of functions previously associated with professional counseling. Many problems traditionally dealt with by counselors are not counseling problems at all, in the sense that special training beyond teaching competence is required. Advisers can handle student scheduling, course selection, some test interpretation and some student problems as well as, or possibly better than, professional counselors.

High school advisement programs seem best organized by clusters with a counselor leading 10 to 12 advisers. Clusters can be arranged by grade levels or across grades depending on preference. Clustering breaks down the impersonal nature of larger schools and enhances communication between counselors and advisers (see Chapter 4).

Many middle schools and some high schools utilize a team teaching approach. When a school is organized by teams, the team organization can be expanded to include advisement by assigning a counselor to several teams and advisement responsibilities to each team member.

The principal and other administrators are also involved. They support the notion that guidance is everyone's responsibility by building advisement time into each teacher's weekly schedule, finding space for advisers to hold individual conferences, and serving as advisers themselves.

School counselors develop a guidance curriculum with essential learnings for all students. The essential learnings are presented in sequence, usually by grade level. Sometimes the essential learnings are presented in large group settings, sometimes by the advisers in advisory group meetings, and sometimes individually in guidance resource centers or the school media center.

The point to remember is that administrators, counselors, and teacher-advisers work in harmony to:

- Deliver the essential learnings of a guidance curriculum;
- Implement a personalized system of instruction geared to the learning needs of each student;
- Support each student's quest for an education connected to individual goals;
- Care for each student;
- Provide a sense of belonging; and
- Reach out to students often overlooked.

CURRENT IMPLEMENTATIONS
AND INTERPRETATIONS

The one concerted effort supporting the inclusion of advisement in school reform can be found in the Coalition of Essential Schools. This project claims membership of over 200 schools. Each school is encouraged to implement the nine principles that focus and guide the project. According to the Coalition's principles, good high schools focus on helping students to:

- ◆ Use their minds well;
- ◆ Keep goals simple;
- ◆ Apply the goals to all students;
- ◆ Personalize teaching and learning;
- ◆ Adopt the metaphor of student-as-worker;
- ◆ Award the diploma upon the successful demonstration of mastery;
- ◆ Stress values of unanxious expectation;
- ◆ Perceive the principal and teachers as generalists first;
- ◆ Maintain manageable class loads; and
- ◆ Allow for substantial planning time.

Although the Coalition is deliberately modest in suggesting practical steps for local implementation, the leadership has encouraged schools to consider student advisory groups in working toward the personalization of teaching and learning.

An early issue of the Coalition's journal, *Horace*, was devoted exclusively to the role advisory groups can play in personalizing students' educational experiences and improving school climate (Cushman, 1990). This issue offered suggestions for descriptions of several advisement programs of Coalition schools. Cushman (1990, p. 1) wrote: "Making a student's education more personal is the base on which the common principles of Essential Schooling stand; and in many schools like these, advisory groupings are emerging as one way to work toward this aim."

This issue was preceded by a trio of books that reported the results of a five-year inquiry into secondary education called *A Study of High School* and essentially served as a basis for the establishment of the Coalition of Essential Schools in 1984. The second book in this series, *The Shopping Mall High School* (Powell, Farrar, & Cohen, 1985) contained over 75 pages of text devoted to teacher advisement programs. The authors noted that student advising in private schools is regarded as an integral duty of the teaching faculty rather than a specialized function of professional counselors. By maintaining a 10:1, adviser:advisee ratio, many private schools are able "to pay particular attention to an individual student" (Powell, Farrar, & Cohen, 1985, p. 220). In the private sector, advisers are not expected to handle deep-seated problems or know counseling techniques. Rather, they are to be ready listeners who communicate with other faculty important information about their charges, attend school events in which advisees are participants, meet with parents as appropriate, and deliver advice in a caring, unthreatening way.

The practice of advising students in private schools is offered as a means to advance the concept of personalization. It is the school's responsibility to find, or to even invent, ways to bring schooling and students in closer proximity. No student wishes to fail. By arranging for all students to be known by at least one adult friend, more comprehensively than is typical of traditionally organized schooling, schools committed to personalizing teaching and learning build academic success into their very fiber. Teacher-advisers care for their advisees, push them to do better, find appropriate help for them when they need it, engage them intellectually and help them see the relationship of formal schooling to improving the quality of one's life.

Middle school advisement has focused mostly on advisory group activities and less on personalizing teaching and learning. Students meet in advisory groups with different activities scheduled for different days. For example, Mondays might be devoted to sustained silent reading. Tuesdays and Wednesdays might be designated sharing and caring where special activities designed by the school counselor(s) or the advisor/advisee coordinator are implemented. Thursdays might be writing-enhancement days where students write letters, journal entries, or essays on assigned topics. Fridays might be option days that include schoolwide projects, administrative directives, intramurals, or school assemblies.

Development of a sense of community and a sense of belonging is emphasized in middle school advisement. By focusing on various developmental tasks of youth, the middle school advisement program addresses the affective education of the middle level student. The developmental tasks for which the adviser/advisee program focuses are:

- ◆ Developing a sense of identity;
- ◆ Developing a sense of responsibility for self and others;
- ◆ Developing appropriate relationships with others;
- ◆ Developing appropriate relationships to institutions and authority; and
- ◆ Developing decision making skills and a sense of independence.

Some middle schools address these tasks by having specific monthly advisement topics, such as study skills; school spirit; self-esteem; social skills; friends; careers; decision making; goal setting; responsibility; and stress management. While academic goals and academic achievement are not ignored at the middle level, they appear ancillary to the affective role of the teacher-advisor. This practice may well be attributed to a belief that when students' affective needs are relatively satisfied, academic achievement is enhanced. This is to say, cognitive learning cannot take place in a state of affective disorder. In fact, many middle school advisement programs are closely aligned with the concept of group guidance.

From its inception the middle-level movement has been concerned with a proper transition between the self-contained nature of the elementary school and the individual nature of the traditional high school. Very often to create a sense of group identity advisory groups adopt different names to separate them from their peers. The groups may remain in tact throughout the middle school years or change each year. Both practices are found in contemporary middle schools.

Some high school advisement programs have adopted the middle school approach. Advisory groups meet from three to five times per week and focus on different content. Others integrate advisement with graduation requirements so that teacher-advisers help advisees create portfolios and exhibitions of their academic accomplishments. The success of any approach to advisement seems only as effective as the commitment, dedication and background of those teachers, staff, and administrators who serve as advisers. Most educators, by virtue of their years of formal schooling and their training, feel competent in dealing one-to-one with students. When the task of delivering a guidance curriculum is added, what is gained initially by the enthusiasm of a new program may wane in the perception that advisement is just another teaching assignment. In fact, many middle and high school programs have lessened their impact as a result of teacher-advisers feeling overwhelmed.

Advisement seems an important consideration to combat a growing alienation between adolescents and formal schooling. Because students appear to benefit from a close, personal relationship with a caring adult, formalized advisement and advocacy programs are one important way to assure that such relationships occur.

2

CONTEXTS: ORGANIZING A SCHOOL FOR ADVISEMENT AND ADVOCACY

Goals 2000 clearly states that every student will master difficult academic subject matter and in the process learn to use his or her mind well. This challenge is unlike any other faced by public schools in recent history. There is no hedging. The word every is unequivocal. Schools can no longer be satisfied with averaged standardized test scores or trumpeting the creative products of a few talented students. Schools must be concerned with each student's accomplishments.

Students bring a variety of backgrounds, interests, aptitudes, and motivations to the school setting. Typical school organizations rarely provide any meaningful context in which to uncover these differences for use in the instructional system. Several models for personalizing education have evolved over the years to enable practitioners to think differently about school structure. One such model evolved from the NASSP Model Schools Project (1969-74). This model, based on the concept of personalized education, used four broad activities: diagnosis, prescription, instruction, and evaluation (DPIE).

James W. Keefe broadened the Model Schools Project interpretation from individualized learning to one of personalized education. Additionally, he embellished the simplified graphic of DPIE depicted in Figure 2.1 to identify working components in each of the four activities.

FIGURE 2.1. FRAMEWORK FOR
PERSONALIZED INSTRUCTION

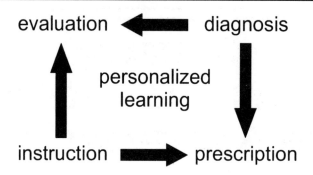

Figure 2.2 redefines the DPIE model to include three sub-components for each activity.

FIGURE 2.2 KEEFE'S MODEL OF
PERSONALIZED INSTRUCTION

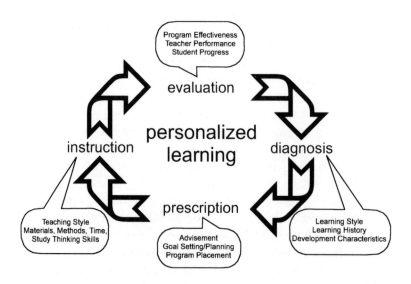

The applicability of the four components of Keefe's model to actual school situations is probably apparent to most educators:

♦ Diagnosis

Teachers often avoid the term "diagnosis" because it appears to imply a complex undertaking. Yet diagnosis is actually a familiar activity in schools everywhere. It is implicit in such statements as, "Her problem is..." and "What he really needs is...." It is important, however, for schools to avoid using the concept of diagnosis to categorize students in negative terms, such as nonreader, exceptional education student, hyperactive, or "in need of remediation." Instead, schools should use the concept of diagnosis in a positive manner, to attempt to discover ways to address each student's:

- Developmental characteristics
- Learning history
- Learning style

♦ Prescription

Just as physicians use prescriptions to help people overcome diagnosed illnesses, teachers should use the prescription process to match students' instruction plans to their assessed needs. These concerns must be addressed to appropriately develop a personalized learning plan:

- Advisement
- Goal setting and planning
- Program placement

♦ Instruction

Some research shows that teachers teach the way they prefer to learn or in accordance with the evaluation system in effect in the school district. Not all students benefit from implementation of one of these two teaching methods. To determine appropriate, personalized instructional methods, teachers must consider these factors:

- Teaching styles
- Teaching methods
- Time use
- Study and thinking skills
◆ Evaluation

Educators must use a variety of authentic measures of student achievement to formulate a personalized educational plan. In schools that successfully use Keefe's model (Figure 2.2, p. 20), students collaborate with classmates and compete with themselves. Group standing is not as relevant in Keefe's model. A valid evaluation must consider:

- Student achievement
- Teacher performance
- Program quality

Personalized education is a systematic effort to take into account individual student characteristics and effective instructional practices in organizing the learning environment. Carroll (1975) calls it:

> ...an attempt to achieve balance between the characteristics of the learner and the learning environment. It is the match of the learning environment with the learner's information, processing strategies, concepts, learning sets, motivational systems achieved and skills acquired. It is a continual process.

Ideally, personalization should tailor teaching to the individual. In practice, personalization of education may take many forms, depending on the available human and instructional resources. There is no "best" method of personalizing education. The DPIE Model forms a context for advisement and advocacy.

ADVISEMENT

Advisement is a key component of personalized education. It is structured to place a professional educator in close proximity of a student over an extended period of time. Usually advisers remain with a small group of advisees for the duration of their time at a particular school. In that way, advisers can get to know each advisee very well in an educational context. The role of teacher-adviser can be cast in four broad categories:

1. Advisers are responsible for a group students small enough to work with each one on a personal basis. The role is different from a conventional homeroom responsibility.

2. Advisers collect information about each advisee from the students, parents, teachers, and outside sources. Information is stored in cumulative folders or computer-based data banks. The data banks contain information about advisee's academic progress, short- and long-range plans of study, list of activities, titles of group and individual projects, autobiographical information, and a record of individual conferences.

3. Advisers help students recognize their personal talents and interests and plan career goals accordingly. Advisers use background and assessment information to advise students about how to use strengths to achieve academic success. They also provide information to teachers about individual advisees.

4. Advisers function as home-base contacts. They contact parents to elicit salient information that can be used to improve learning environments for individual students. Sometimes they visit the homes of advisees as part of this process. In many respects, advisers are an extension of the family. It is not unusual for an adviser to be invited to family functions as the adviser interacts with individual students over a school career.

The ratio of advisees to adviser is a critical factor in combating the ill effects of bigness. Every student is viewed as important and is given the recognition that accompanies a listening ear on the part of an adult mentor who cares. President and Mrs.

Clinton recently acknowledged the work of nine large high schools that had succeeded in keeping students from getting in trouble. A student in one of these schools with 5000-plus students remarked that as soon as he came to the school and got in trouble for the first time, the faculty would not leave him alone. He said, "They made me take part in activities and involved me in various groups. An assistant principal became my mentor and has become one of my best friends." The student, a member of a school gang at age 12, now splits his time volunteering as a Little League coach, working as a school guard at lunch time, and helping out as a clerk in the school office. He maintains a B average and hopes to go to college after graduation this year (Rivera-Lyles, 1998). The negative in this scenario is that the student had to get in trouble in order to receive personal attention.

Unfortunately, the current status of too many schools makes such examples the exception rather than the rule. Large schools produce anonymity for many students. Getting lost in the numbers, students often connect with negative influences and are rarely encouraged to advance beyond their current station in life. The personal touch offered by advisement programs and individual staff members who care is not found in many places. School structures frequently preclude such behavior. Sir Winston Churchill's statement, "We shape our institutions and then they shape us," seems a fitting commentary on the situations that plague many schools. Every student needs to have one or more adult friends who care what happens to him or her and who intervenes when appropriate.

ORGANIZATIONAL OPTIONS TO ADVISEMENT

LEARNING COMMUNITIES

Keefe and Jenkins (1997) contend that the establishment of a school learning community is necessary if a school is to become a total learning organization. Lee, Croninger, and Smith (1995) studied the characteristics of high schools as learning communities. They found that when schools take collective responsibility for student learning, gains in student achievement occur. Kruse and Seashore Louis (1995) report that among the conditions that support the development of learning communities are small size, physical proximity, and team teaching.

On a macroscopic level, a learning community defines an entire school. On a smaller scale, a learning community can be a team of professionals committed to serving a prescribed number of students well, usually over an extended period of time. The Advancement Lab, a program at Wilde Lake High School in the 1970s, served students who were judged to be "at risk." The 20 students assigned to the program had a history of school failure and displayed extreme difficulty in taking responsibility for their academic and social behavior. One and one-half teachers, a full-time teacher aide, and a part-time guidance counselor staffed the program. The students were scheduled with the team for the major portion of the school day (four to five hours). A student remained in the Lab until the team concluded that the student was ready to take his or her place in the school proper. Credits toward graduation were earned through completing coursework and projects in the Lab environment. In some cases, the students were scheduled outside the Lab for specific learning activities, such as physical education and reading resource. The team members met daily to plan and discuss individual student progress. They became the authorities on the learning and social needs of each student assigned to the Lab.

The Advancement Lab was a precursor to the ALPS (Alternative Learning Program) in the Howard County, Maryland, public schools. This program exists in four of the six high schools and focuses on the needs of students likely to leave school before graduation. The program serves approximately 75 students per school and is staffed by one teacher and teacher aide. At Wilde Lake High School, the ALPS staff was joined by the teacher in the "contract room," a place for students referred by one or more teachers because of behavioral problems. By scheduling the programs in adjacent rooms, the teachers were able to work together to the benefit of more students. The two teachers and an aide served approximately 20 to 22 students each class period. The small student-teacher ratio and the time the team and the students had together enabled teaching and learning to become more personalized.

William Glasser (1997) describes a program at the Schwab Middle School in Cincinnati, Ohio, in which 170 students who had failed at least one grade and attended regularly were enrolled. Seven teachers from the regular school staff volunteered for the program. The Cambridge Program, as it was called, was created by the teachers and catered to the interests and needs of the students. Spurred by the freedom to do what they thought best for the students, the teachers worked day and night for almost two months to devise lessons in which students had to demonstrate that they could read, write, solve problems, and learn the basics of social studies and science. Additionally, "choice theory" (see Chapter 6) was employed to help teachers learn how to help students value school experiences and make better decisions. The teachers stopped using coercion as a means to control students. In its place, they substituted ways to enable students to satisfy their psychological needs. Students responded positively. Achievement improved markedly, and discipline problems were minimized. When asked why they were no longer disruptive and why they were beginning to work in school, the students said, "You care about us." And sometimes they added, "And now you give us choices and work we like to do" (Glasser, 1997, p. 601).

TEAMING

Teaming refers to assembling a group of teachers from different disciplines and/or grade levels who work together as a "core group" responsible for teaching a subset of the schools population (Kruse & Seashore Louis, 1995). The interdisciplinary team is more likely to be found at the middle level than at any others. Students are grouped for a block of time, typically three to four periods, with the same team. The team may remain with the students throughout their middle school years or change each year depending on the philosophy of the school. The idea is to create small, stable communities of learning, where teachers respond to the emotional, social, and educational needs of early adolescents. In 1989, the Carnegie Council on Adolescent Development said teacher teams provide "an environment conducive to learning by reducing the stress of anonymity and isolation of students." When the number of students assigned to a team is manageable, teachers can know students more intimately, which knowledge provides a more personalized approach to learning.

Teams frequently share common physical space, either several regular classrooms, a large open area, or a combination of arrangements for large group meetings, small group work, and independent pursuits. Team configurations include teachers from the core subjects of mathematics, language arts, science, and social studies. Sometimes, a teacher of special education is added to assist with inclusion efforts or to serve as a resource for the team in augmenting diagnosed weaknesses in cognitive processing skills. Teams meet formally each day to plan curriculum and instruction and to monitor the progress of particular students. Individual teachers on the teams often serve as advisers or advocates for a smaller segment of students within the teaming structure. The teaming arrangement enables teachers to take a broader approach to the emotional and educational needs of each student. Kruse and Seashore-Louis (1995) found that teachers on teams often said they were motivated to work hard to meet the needs of "our kids."

HOUSE PLANS, ACADEMIES, OR SCHOOLS-WITHIN-SCHOOLS

Yale University assigns its undergraduate population to 12 residential colleges. Each college has approximately 400 students and is staffed by a house master and a dean. Upperclass students, sophomores through seniors, live together in the college residence with the live-in house master. Each residential college has a dining hall. Freshmen are assigned to a separate dormitory, but eat their meals at the residential dining hall affiliated with their college. Commencement exercises are held for the entire university and at each residential college. The college graduations are small and personal. Each graduate is introduced by the Dean as he or she steps forward to receive a diploma. The house plan at Yale keeps students together where they can make friends more easily, receive counsel as needed on a personal basis, and feel a part of a larger, prestigious university.

At Patterson High School, Baltimore, Maryland, upper-level students choose to attend one of five teacher-led academies focused on career orientation. Ninth graders are assigned to the Ninth Grade Success Academy. The five career academies are Arts and Humanities, Business and Finance, Environmental Sciences and Aquatic Studies, Sports Studies and Health/Wellness, and Transportation and Engineering. Each academy enrolls between 250 and 350 students and has its own faculty of 14 to 18 teachers, a principal, an academy leader (often a former department head), and a guidance counselor. The Ninth Grade Academy is composed of five teams with four or five teachers on each team. Teams share the same 150 to 200 students and help individual students with their problems.

Teams share a common planning period to plan curriculum and discuss the progress of individual students. In all six academies, teachers take responsibility for helping individual students. It is not uncommon for them to call at least two students each day who are absent from school to inquire about their health and to encourage their return to school. This type of personalization has improved the climate for learning throughout the 2000-student high school. Surveys by the researchers from Johns Hopkins University Center for Research on the Education of Students At Risk show that before the academies were created, 85 percent of the faculty agreed that "the environment of this school is not conducive to learning." Now, 10 agree. Before the academies, only 13 percent agreed that, "this school seems like a big family, everyone is close and cordial." Now, 67 percent agree (McPartland, Jordan, Legters, & Balfanz, 1997). Students also agree that the academies have made a difference. They like the opportunity to choose a curriculum centered on their interests. Students also find the small numbers to be an antidote to the anonymity that is typical in large schools. This perception is captured in the 1996 observation of Wendy Ramirez, a twelfth grade student: "Teachers seem like they care now" (Viadero, 1996). Three years later, they seem to care even more. The smallness of each academy has enabled teachers to get to know the students very well.

Fenway Middle College High Pilot School, Boston, Massachusetts, is divided into three different houses. Each house has a distinct character and its own community collaborations, which shape the nature of the house. One house focuses on a pre-pharmacy career development program, a second on allied health professions, and the third on a range of potential careers including community service. Collaborative partnerships are arranged with community-based firms such as CVS Pharmacies, Lotus Corporation, and the Children's Hospital. The house plan has two purposes: First, to unite students in grades 9 to 12 in a group of 60 students as part of one or more collaboratives. Second, to maintain the teachers' ability to know the students well and preserves the personal attention students receive by limiting the number of students to 60 per collaborative. Students work closely with teachers at the school and with mentors in the community.

The New York City Board of Education launched more than 50 small new-model high schools between 1992 and 1995. In 1995, the Center for Collaborative Education, as part of an Annenberg grant to recreate schools in several urban areas in the United States, undertook to establish an additional 50 new small schools. Large high school buildings were subdivided into several smaller independent schools. One such school, the Julia Richmond High School, became 4 schools of 600 students each (Darling-Hammond, 1997). The new smaller high schools range in size from 300 to 600 students. Deborah Meier, formerly principal of the Central Park East Secondary School, one of the initial small high schools and the model for many that followed, honors the following values in small high schools: "In small schools...every kid is known, every kid belongs to a community that includes adults. Relationships are cross-disciplinary, cross-generational, and cross-everything else....In small schools, we're more likely to pass on to students the habits of heart and mind that define an educated person—not only formally, in lesson plans and pedagogical gimmicks, but in hallway exchanges, arguments about important matters, and resolution of ordinary differences" (Meier, 1996, p. 14). The fact that there are more winners in small schools seems clear. Large high schools create anonymity. Smaller high schools generate a sense of belonging for more students.

Mary Ann Raywid's (1998) synthesis of the research on small schools seems instructive in this regard. In reviewing over 40 separate studies, she found:

- Students at all grade levels learn more in small schools than in large schools.
- At-risk students are much more likely to succeed in small schools than large schools.
- Small schools are far more likely to be violence-free than large schools.
- The bonds created in small schools enable such schools to influence students' post-high school behavior, including college attendance.

The success of small schools is attributable to various features, all of which seem to emerge from three key factors:

- Small size;
- An unconventional structure; and
- A setting that operates more like a community than a bureaucracy.

The Commission on the Restructuring of the American High School, that produced the publication *Breaking Ranks* (1996), recommended that "each high school should try to limit its enrollment to self-operating units of no more than 600 students." They wrote, "smallness of scale can be created in many ways, even in a structure built to accommodate a large enrollment. House plans and cluster programs...group students into smaller, more intimate units. Such approaches seek to reduce the number of teachers and other students with whom a student comes in contact each day. An organizational approach that produced some kind of school-within-a-school moves toward combating the bigness that shrouds so many youngsters in a cloak of anonymity" (p. 46).

LOOPING

Looping, which is sometimes called multiyear teaching or multiyear placement, positions a teacher with the same students for more than one year. Looping's growing popularity is found mostly at the primary level in the elementary school but also has implications for middle and high schools. In essence, when looping occurs, a teacher is promoted with his or her students. The advantages appear obvious. More time for teaching is achieved when teachers do not have to spend time at the beginning of the year establishing routines and classroom expectations. This time can be used to build or extend a sense of community. Additionally, information a teacher has gleaned over a full year with students is not lost in codification for cumulative records or communicated to other teachers in passing. A first and second grade teacher at an elementary school in Colorado made the following observation (during the summer): "I think about certain children who are having behavior or academic problems and ask myself, 'What can I do to help this child?' ...You don't have to start from scratch with each child" (Rasmussen, 1998, p. 2). Looping also facilitates parent involvement. Parents and teachers develop a deeper relationship that fosters cooperation in helping students.

In a study of the effects of looping, Simel (1998) found the biggest advantage to looping was the family atmosphere that was created in a looped classroom. One surveyed teacher remarked, "This group has formed a family....They help each other to the point that it is just amazing...and they feed on this." Another said that the "sense of family was a big difference from any other class that I've had" (p. 334). At-risk students especially benefit from the secure feeling that a family atmosphere at school imbues. Many of these children's parents work two jobs or are single parents. The bonds established with the teacher and other students are invaluable.

Looping can be applied at the secondary level by having teachers advance to the next course in a sequenced curriculum with the same students. Usually this is harder to do at the high school level where many uncontrollable variables impinge on the master schedule. It is not impossible, however, and some teachers have extolled the virtues of having the same students for two and three years of English or mathematics. Because the teachers are not with these students the entire school day, the benefits are not as great, but nevertheless they exist.

The concept of looping is found historically in the nongraded movement in the United States where teams of teachers and students formed a primary block or intermediate block. In nongraded elementary schools, children remained with the same team for up to three years. The length of stay permitted teachers the opportunity to work individually with students and to delay decisions of promotion or retention. Interestingly, looping has been practiced for years in schools in Germany and Japan (Simel, 1998).

Related to looping is the relatively new high school scheduling practice of reducing the number of classes, thus students that a teacher sees in a day, a week and a semester. The 4×4 schedule reduces the number of classes a student takes each semester and the number of students a teachers is responsible to teaching. Students enroll in four classes rather than the traditional, six or seven; teachers teach three classes rather than five or six. This arrangement decreases the number of students a teacher must know from approximately 150 to 80 or 90. The smaller number facilitates a closer working relationship between teachers and students. Obviously, this approach isn't as personal as some of the other reform efforts, but it seems to be a step in that direction.

THE RELATIONSHIP OF ADVISEMENT TO OTHER STRUCTURES

All students need the help of a caring adult who is aware of their strengths, weaknesses, interests, and unique development. The image of Mark Hopkins at the end of one log and James Garfield, his student, at the other end may evoke a desire to replicate a one-to-one relationship between students and their teachers that is hardly feasible given the level of funding of today's public schools or the nature of most school structures. The DPIE model of personalized education includes advisement as a component of prescription. The adviser is viewed as the one person in a school who knows most about an advisee in order to personalize the total educational experience. When education is personalized, more students have a chance to succeed in school and find reasons to stay the course of 12 years of schooling. The key to getting to know students as "total human beings educationally," as the late J. Lloyd Trump suggested, is to have few students to get to know and the sufficient time in which to do it. Whether a school establishes a formal advisory program, as we recommend, or implements one of the other structural changes to bring students and teachers closer together seems a matter of choice. What is important is that each student gains a sense of belonging and finds one adult in which he or she can trust. In the words of Ted Sizer, founder of the Coalition of Essential Schools and the co-headmaster of the Francis Parker Charter School in Massachusetts, "For too many American young people school is the last, best sanctuary, the one place where a student can trust that an adult is concerned for him or her."

3

QUALITY
EXEMPLARS

For some middle and high schools the present is merely pro-logue. These nine schools have taken additional steps to restore the importance of education to the internal value system of all of their students. The advisement programs in these schools seem a cut above the rest and serve as beacons for educational reform in the new century. Each of these nine schools possesses a collection of positive attributes which is unequaled by other schools in the U.S. and Canada.

While each of these outstanding schools is unique, there are several traits shared by all. One unifying thread is longevity. The only exception began as a new school six years ago with a specific program design in mind. Their advisement program was built upon the best of the past and has evolved over the six-year period to support their unique approach to personalized learning.

BISHOP CARROLL HIGH SCHOOL

4624 Richard Road, SW
Calgary, Alberta T3E-6L1, Canada
(403) 249-6601

Bishop Carroll was one of the original high schools in the NASSP Model Schools Project (1969-74). It joined the Model Schools network on its opening in 1971. The building was actually constructed to support all of the various components prescribed by the Model Schools Project. As a result, individual offices for teachers were built to support the teacher-adviser component. If teacher-advisers were to meet on an individual basis with advisees, they needed an appropriate place in which to do so.

Teacher-advisers spend a significant amount of time individually with advisees. Each teacher serves 20 to 35 students from all grade levels. Students are assigned to advisers when they enter the school and remain with them until graduation. New students are assigned to open slots in advisement groups each year.

Teacher-advisers and advisees maintain continuous contact. At the beginning of each school year, teacher-advisers meet individually with advisees to plan personalized schedules for the year. Additional meetings are scheduled at least once a month for grade 11 and 12 students to review academic progress, diagnose problems, and prescribe solutions. Grade 10 students meet with their advisers every two weeks throughout the year. All members of the advisory group meet briefly at the beginning and end of each school day to take attendance and to schedule individual conferences. Teacher-advisers are specifically responsible for monitoring student attendance, academic progress and participation in school activities. They also oversee the records of student accomplishment. Questions dealing with any students are handled first by the teacher-adviser who may refer the inquiry to a counselor, parent or administrator.

A close relationship develops between the adviser and advisees. Teacher-advisers serve as mentors, assisting advisees with school adjustment problems, referring them to subject teachers for special help and providing support as students work through their personal learning plans (Keefe, 1983).

Bishop Carroll is a unique school. Students progress at their own rate of speed through a continuous progress program of curriculum and instruction. This means that students may earn more credits in a typical year than is true of a traditional high school, or they can take longer in earning credits. The teacher-adviser monitors the process carefully, intervening when necessary to keep individual advisees on track and to suggest changes when apropos. The role of the teacher-adviser is critical to the success of the school's continuous progress program of education. Students may enter school or graduate from school during any month of the school year.

Students with the help of their teacher-advisers determine the number of times per week they will spend in each of nine subject areas (English, mathematics, social studies, science, other cultures, fine arts, practical arts, physical education, and religion). To help advisees in the course selection process, the advisers must know the courses and the course requirements in all areas.

The school's unique approach to instruction and student scheduling enables teacher-advisers to meet with individual advisees throughout the school day or when a need arises. As a rule, teachers are scheduled with students in an instructional setting approximately 25 hours every 2 weeks. A portion of the teachers' unscheduled time is used to meet the responsibilities of being an adviser.

The success of the Bishop Carroll program is discernible from its longevity and from the numbers of graduates who have succeeded at the university level, in the work world and in life.

CENTRAL PARK EAST
SECONDARY SCHOOL (CPESS)

1573 Madison Avenue
New York, NY 10029
(212) 860-8935

Central Park East is a small, secondary school that serves 450 students in grades 7 to 12. The students are drawn largely from the local community. Over 75 percent of the students are of Hispanic or African descent. Greater than 60 percent of the students qualify for free or reduced lunch. The school has been affiliated with the Coalition of Essential Schools since its inception (Darling-Hammond & Ancess, 1994).

All students belong to a 12- to 15-member advisory group. They remain with the same adviser for two years, corresponding to the years spent in each of the school's three divisions. Division I corresponds to grades 7 and 8, division II corresponds to grades 9 and 10, and the Senior Institute approximates grades 11 and 12. Advisers meet with their advisory groups for an hour each day to discuss school and community issues. All professional staff members serve as advisers.

The advisory period is used as study time, an opportunity for quiet reading, writing, discussion of health, social and ethical issues, and for one-on-one conferences. The adviser is the "expert" on the student, meeting frequently with the family and with other teachers to ensure communication about the student's needs and progress and to guide the student through courses and graduation requirements (Darling-Hammond & Ancess, 1994, pp. 9–10).

The Senior Institute adviser meets individually with advisees to develop a postgraduation plan, which is later discussed with the advisees' families. The plan includes a time line of the student's key life events from birth to date and continuing 10 years into the future. The students examine career possibilities, and research colleges and universities and internship placements. At Central Park East community internships are a key part of a student's education. Teacher-advisers arrange visits to colleges and help advisees enroll in college courses while still in high school. Educators at CPESS believe that direct experiences with college level courses on a college campus provide students with a much better insight into their suitability for higher education than traditional test scores.

CPESS focuses on developing a learning environment that permits students to construct their own knowledge, develop their capacities for independent reasoning and develop habits of mind that enable them to be competent citizens. Traditional credit requirements for graduation are replaced by a portfolio system. Students are required to present portfolios in each of 14 areas to demonstrate what they have learned during their 6 or sometimes 7 years at the school. Portfolios cover such topics as an autobiography, a postgraduate plan, the community internship and service, ethics and social issues, mass media, as well as traditional subject areas. In addition, each graduate must complete a project in an area of interest. Seven portfolios are presented orally before a graduation committee that includes the student's adviser, and seven are submitted for independent evaluation.

Senior Institute teachers spend about half their time advising students rather than teaching classes. They are scheduled for 12 hours per week of formal teaching and the remainder of their time is devoted to advisory groups, working with individual advisees on portfolio development and serving on advisee graduation committees.

FREEDOM HIGH SCHOOL

2332 San Mateo Place, NE
Albuquerque, NM 87110-4051
(505) 884-6012

Freedom High School established an advisement program in 1971, one year after the school opened. The school is an educational alternative for students at risk of dropping out of the traditional high school. The school enrolls 220 students in grades 11 and 12 and has a waiting list for students wanting to enter the program. To apply for admission, a student must have a minimum of 10 credits, an official transcript, and a counselor's referral from the home school. When a student enrolls, the student is assigned to a faculty member who serves as an adviser, assisting in scheduling and evaluating the student's progress.

Each member of the professional staff is assigned advisement responsibilities for 22 students. Advisers monitor the academic and social progress of their advisees. Advisers meet once per week with their advisory groups for a period of 20 minutes. They keep up with all aspects of school life in an individualized and personal setting. Individual conferences are held with advisees on a regular basis. Advisers monitor student attendance carefully and serve as a member of all staffing committees involving their advisees.

Teachers notify the advisers of advisees who are not progressing well academically. Advisers then confer with the advisee to help create a plan to address the problem. The plan may include a change of schedule, meetings with the advisee's parents, motivational strategies, or a combination of any of these. The progress of every student is important at Freedom High School. No student is permitted to "fall through the cracks." Advisers also oversee advisees' work placements outside of school. They visit their work sites and maintain regular communication with employees.

Advisers have time during the regular school day on Wednesday and Friday afternoon to conduct advisee business, including updating personal records. As the winter recess nears, the entire school, through the adviser system, conducts what is called a "celebration of living." Here, students converse with their advisers and other advisees in their group about problems that might be encountered over the holidays, and what they can do about them.

Advisers communicate regularly with parents about academics and behavior. The goal is to help each student meet the graduation requirements for a diploma while learning skills needed for success in the new century. Advisers are perceived as advocates for their advisees.

MCCLUER NORTH HIGH SCHOOL

705 Waterford Drive
Florissant, MO 63033
(314) 831-6600

The advisement program at McCluer North was begun during the 1971-72 school year, with the opening of a new high school. It was established to offer students assistance in developing programs of study that would fit their own needs rather than forcing them to fit a traditional program.

The curriculum also needed the advisement system. The courses were designed on the assumption that students would find schedules that were exactly right for them. Advisement functions as the primary means by which the school responds to its students—personally, systematically, and purposefully.

A contributing factor to the success of the advisement program is a staff that cares a great deal about the students as human beings, believes in their essential goodness, and trusts them. Each staff member, including administrators, is an adviser to approximately 16 students. All, regardless of their special roles, attempt to relate students and parents on a personal basis. A common commitment ensures that all persons and groups share responsibility for advisement's successful operation.

Ideally, student and parents should choose the advisers they believe understands them best and can give the help they need. During the registration period, prior to entering high school, eighth grade students and parents are asked to name an adviser they prefer. Many students were able to request advisers based on other sibling's experiences or recommendations from other families or students.

Those students not able to specify an adviser are asked to indicate criteria—sex, age, interests, or subject taught—that can be used by the registrar for initial assignment.

After students have completed a semester, they and their parents have an opportunity to request a change in adviser. A form is signed by the current adviser and by the adviser requested, who indicates a willingness to accept another advisee. The records are then transferred.

The advisement system allows time for each adviser to meet individually or in group settings with advisees. Every adviser has two hours of released time weekly for conducting individual conferences. In addition, advisory groups meet every Monday for 15 minutes between the first and second period so that advisers can disseminate information to the entire group.

Several times during the year, especially during registration, parents are invited to participate in conferences to help formulate plans and to be involved in the decision-making process.

Advisers have access to all student records. With these data, they are able to audit graduation requirements and help their advisees stay focused on their goals. Advisers also regularly request assistance from guidance counselors.

Goals for advisement are clearly defined. Specific tasks and activities are identified and categorized as follows:

- Program planning—assisting students in selecting courses, evaluating courses and developing long-range plans.
- School offerings—increasing student awareness of school programs, services and operations.
- Self-assessment—helping students understand their own behavior, identifying strengths and weaknesses and setting goals.
- Parent relations/conferences—increasing parent participation in educational and career planning for their children.
- School/community issues—helping members of the school community understand and solve problems, such as problems involving vandalism or race relations.
- Feedback/evaluation—collecting information about the school, formally and informally, that can be used to improve programs and operations.
- Career planning/preparation—assisting students in exploring career options and preparing for careers.

♦ Decision making—applying the principles of sound decision making to the tasks of advisement.

Some adjustments are made for advisement. The role of the professional counselor is redefined in a way that complements the advisement system. Counselors do not spend the major portion of the day working with large numbers of students. They use their special training to serve a variety of needs and to be facilitators of the advisement program. Because they serve as advisers also, they assume ownership and benefit from the information-sharing that takes place among all colleagues.

With advisement the school's goals belong to everyone. When everyone respects the school's goals, philosophy, priorities, and focus on improving human relations, the total school environment is significantly improved.

METRO HIGH SCHOOL

1212 7th Street
Cedar Rapids, IA 52404
(319) 398-2193

Metro High School offers an educational alternative for students in Cedar Rapids, Iowa. The majority of the 450 students who choose to attend Metro have had unsuccessful experiences in previous schools and usually harbor negative attitudes toward the educational system. Many of the students have jobs, have babies who they bring to the school's day care center, and face grinding personal challenges at home. Consequently, a conscious effort is made to provide a relaxed, supportive, and caring atmosphere. Each student is recognized and accepted as an individual with unique interests, abilities and learning styles.

The heart of the school is the advisory and advocacy system. Each teacher (40 total) serves as an adviser for 15 students. The system is designed to assist students in their school performance and to help with their personal lives. Advisers meet with parents, guardians, and significant others throughout each trimester.

Once assigned to a student, the adviser remains the same throughout the student's enrollment. Advisers meet with their advisees in monthly advisory group meetings, individually during the school day, and on Fridays in their homes. The adviser system is designed to provide maximum support to the students and assistance to the parents/guardians.

A unique feature of the Metro system happens each Friday. No classes meet. Many students are at work that the school helped to arrange, or in community placements associated with the school curriculum. Following a morning staff meeting, teacher advisers visit the homes of four or five advisees to talk with the parent(s) and the advisee, or to talk with the advisee in a different setting. Usually the advisers travel in pairs to gain different perspectives and sometimes for safety. Fridays also facilitate field trips of and meetings of advisory groups or other special groupings. For example, this past year a student men's group and a student women's group met regularly at the school on Fridays to discuss common interests and issues.

The adviser's role at Metro encompasses behavior management, as well as educational planning, career development, and guidance in work placement. Advisers work with probation officers and social service agencies. The teacher-adviser is the student's strongest advocate and most important link to the school.

When students enter Metro, they go through an extensive orientation program. It is a week-long course that helps them assess their academic skills and learning styles, learn appropriate behavioral expectations, and become acquainted with the school culture. At the end of the week, students are assigned an adviser. Every attempt is made to match the student with a suitable teacher-adviser and advisory group. As part of the orientation program, students write an autobiography for placement in their portfolios. The student portfolio is a chronicle of academic and community works at the school. Teacher-advisers work with their advisees each term to keep the portfolios current.

Metro has been honored by *Redbook* magazine as one of the top 140 schools in the United States and has twice received recognition as a Blue Ribbon school. It is also a member of the Coalition of Essential Schools. The following statement from the school's current principal captures the spirit that pervades the school campus:

> At Metro, teachers and associates operate well beyond the walls of Metro High School. They make an incredible number of phone calls and home visits to help our students. They take students to lunch, to visit colleges, to court, to medical appointments, and to cleanup projects. They go on canoe trips and bicycle trips, to banquets, and to weekend activities at the University of Iowa. They serve as counselors, social workers, chauffeurs, friends, and, most of all, as strong advocates for Metro students.

NEW TRIER TOWNSHIP
HIGH SCHOOL

385 Winnetka Avenue
Winnetka, IL 60093
(708) 446-7000

New Trier has the nation's longest running advisement program. Beginning in 1924, advisement is viewed as crucial to achieving the school's belief that "everyone is special." It is especially important in a school with approximately 3800 students in grades 9 to 12. The advisement program provides an individualized and humane means for monitoring the academic progress of each student constructively.

Each student is assigned a teacher-adviser upon entering the school, usually at grade 9. The adviser remains with the student throughout the student's career at New Trier. Changes in advisers are made only when it is judged in the best interest of the student and are rare. During a student's ninth grade year, teacher-advisers visit the homes of each advisee and meet the family. The adviser and the family remain in close contact for the next four years.

Functions of the advisement program are grouped in four categories: *personal adjustment,* which includes orientation to the school and aid in physical, social, emotional, and scholastic adjustment; *guidance,* which includes curriculum planning and vocational and college preparation and advice; *communication* with students, parents, and teachers; and *administration,* which includes processing records and reports.

Teacher schedules are adjusted so that advisement constitutes one-fifth of a teacher's teaching responsibilities. Teacher-advisers meet each morning for 25 minutes with their advisory groups of 25 to 30 students. They develop a sense of rapport and responsibility for their advisees and their personal and academic progress. They are usually the first person a parent or faculty member contacts for information and advice. Advisers serve as adult role models for their advisees, and their perspective on each advisee is highly regarded.

On the surface, the advisory group meetings look similar to the old homeroom concept. The main difference, however, is in the continuing contact that advisers have with advisees and with the relationships that advisers establish with individual advisees. Teacher-advisers are perceived as friends and confidantes, and even surrogate parents, at times. As one teacher observed, "The adviser room is the key to New Trier's success because it keeps the school from being an anonymous place" (Maeroff, 1986, p. 182).

Advisers take attendance each day and call home when a student is absent. They schedule a formal conference with the parents of each advisee once per year. Individual conferences with advisees, and sometimes parents, are arranged as needed. Advisers write letters of recommendation for advisees, and provide counselors with evaluations and insights into the characteristics of each advisee. Course selection and program planning all emanate with the students' teacher-advisers. "Of all people with whom the student deals at school, the adviser exercises the greatest influence on the student during his (her) four years at New Trier" (*Student Guide Book*, 1990-91, p. 4).

The Director of Student Services has administrative responsibility for the advisement program. Two adviser chairpersons for each class, a total of eight, direct the work of the individual advisers. The chairpersons are specialists in the grade level they serve, and plan and conduct inservice workshops for the advisers. They also meet with advisers individually to help with specific tasks or problems.

The adviser chairpersons provide advisers with weekly notes on advisory group procedures, review the course planning and registration of the students, handle all disciplinary referrals for their class groups, and plan class activities for their respective advisory groups.

Four keys to the success of the New Trier advisement system are the quality of teacher-adviser, the time provided in each adviser's schedule to meet the responsibilities of advisement, the support advisers receive from counselors, grade-level chairpersons, and administrators, and the commitment of the staff to individualized learning and personalizing the process of education.

In a large school such as New Trier, the advisory group is an antidote to anonymity, a home away from home. It is a comfort for students to begin each day with a mentor in whom they can confide, and an advocate on whom they can rely for support and advice (Jenkins, 1992, p. 27).

THOMAS HANEY
SECONDARY SCHOOL (THSS)

23000-116 Avenue
Maple Ridge, British Columbia V2X-0T8, Canada
(604) 463-2001

Thomas Haney is a grade 9 to 12 secondary school located in a suburb of Vancouver, British Columbia. There are 875 students attending the school. The school opened in 1992 using a directed, self-paced model of instruction with one of its founding pillars being a strong teacher-adviser program. All full-time teaching staff, including administrators and counselors, serve as teacher-advisers. Currently, 41 teachers, two administrators, including the principal, and four other professional staff members serve as advisers. Students usually remain with their advisers all five years they attend the school. They may change by making application with a counselor who processes the request in consultation with the current adviser, the requested adviser, the parent, and the student.

Advisory groups are typically composed of 20 students and are multiage and family based. (The latter refers to the practice of assigning siblings to the same adviser.) When a student moves or graduates, new students are assigned randomly to fill the vacancies. Each year with student growth, two or three new advisory groups are formed by asking for student volunteers. Because these new groups are assigned to new teachers, they are kept smaller during the initial year.

The students meet as a group with their advisers 10 times each week. On Monday and Thursday, meetings are scheduled for one hour. On Tuesday, Wednesday, and Friday, meetings are scheduled for 15 minutes. Advisory groups meet for five minutes after lunch every day. The one-hour meeting on Monday enables the advisers to work with their advisees to set goals for the week, develop plans, and arrange student schedules. The one-hour meeting on Thursday enables advisers to check each advisee's academic progress.

The teacher-advisers are the primary contact between the home and the school, and their advocacy role allows for close monitoring of all students. There is always one adult in the school who has close personal knowledge of all facets of a student's academic life and some facets of a student's personal life. Teacher-advisers also become aware of the learning styles of their advisees and encourage them to plan or negotiate activities with their teachers that reflect the most appropriate use of their learning style profiles. For purposes of first-level diagnosis, the school uses the Learning Style Profile developed and published by the National Association of Secondary School Principals. (The use of this instrument is described in Chapter 5.) With the use of a computer management system and a paper tracking system, teacher-advisers are always in touch with student progress. Formal individual student conferences are officially scheduled once per year but are regularly scheduled throughout the year as advisers work closely with advisees. Reports to parents occur three times per year, but most advisers report academic progress monthly.

After six years it is apparent that the teacher-adviser system is the single most powerful program at Thomas Haney. Directed, self-paced learning leads to success for all students, but it is the coaching that comes from the teacher-advisers that contributes most to the high academic success rate. Parents indicate positive support for the advisement program.

The relationship of student to teacher-adviser to parent is described as triangular. The student is at the apex of the triangle with advisers, teachers and parents in supporting roles. The school's goal is to produce self-sufficient and responsible learners.

SHOREHAM-WADING RIVER MIDDLE SCHOOL

Randall Road
Shoreham, NY 11786
(516) 821-8210

Shoreham-Wading River Middle School built its entire program around the concept of advisement, a system that emphasizes support and advocacy for each student. To this end, the school is divided into advisory groups of 12 students each. All teachers and administrators serve as advisers. The groups meet for 12 minutes each morning, as a substitute for the traditional homeroom, and at lunchtime. Advisees meet at the adviser's classroom to eat lunch together or go to a local fast-food establishment accompanied by their adviser.

An early morning bus run is provided on Mondays through Thursdays so that teacher-advisers can confer with individual advisees. The individual conference has been described as "the crown jewel" of the advisory system (Maeroff, 1990). Other students remain at home until the regular bus run, or come to practice with one of the music groups, or go to the gymnasium with the physical education teachers. On Fridays, four or five advisers of a particular academic team meet to discuss their students and exchange information about them.

Advisory groups are heterogeneous and include both special education students and nonclassified students. In the sixth grade, teacher advisers deal with entire classes of 25. In the seventh and eighth grades, the school is structured so that four or five teacher-advisers share 50 students. The morning conference time, however, is consistent across all three grades.

Advisers are advocates for their advisees, but do not perceive themselves as surrogate parents. Students change their advisers each year. At the end of sixth grade, advisers place their students in seventh grade advisories; seventh grade advisers do the same for their advisees as they move to the eighth grade. Placement is accomplished by considering the needs, interests, and peer relationships of the individual advisee along with the strengths of particular teacher-advisers. At the sixth grade, the self-contained classroom organization is also the advisory.

An adviser's responsibility is to know the students and their families, their interests, their strengths and weaknesses and their day-to-day experiences. One-on-one conferences are regularly planned conversations between the advisers and their advisees, and the two daily group meetings likewise involve conversation, discussion of school events, or relaxation and fun.

Teacher-advisers and their advisees plan a variety of activities, such as pizza lunches, birthday parties, trips to movies, concerts or ball games, skits for the annual school variety show, and food drives for needy families. Advisory group discussions focus on put-downs, anger, victimization, problems in classes, homework, and test taking.

Parents meet with advisers during the fall open house. Report cards and other information flow from the teachers to the advisers, who prepare report cards and hold parent conferences during the two days scheduled for this purpose. Advisers routinely handle telephone calls from or to parents.

Classroom teachers go to a student's adviser first about issues of concern, such as missed homework, deficient academic progress, tension with another student or the possibility of a crisis at home. The adviser's relationship with the advisees is such that if the adviser discerns a pattern of behavior, the adviser speaks with the student and/or parent, asks the guidance counselor for advice or help, and meets with the student as needed. A child-study team serves as a resource for the advisers.

The atmosphere in the school is warm, positive, lively, and appropriate for early adolescents. Advisers handle much of the discipline. Students are referred to administrators in rare cases of repeated or extreme misbehavior (Jenkins, 1997). Having an adviser means that each student has an adult in the school to whom the student can turn. Much of the success of the school program is attributed to the advisory system.

WAKULLA MIDDLE SCHOOL

22 Jenn Drive
Crawfordville, FL 32327
(850) 926-7143

The advisement program at Wakulla Middle School is a combination of small-group guidance conducted by each teacher, and classroom guidance delivered by the guidance counselor. The class meets on the same day each week all year long. Teachers divide their homerooms into three small groups of 10 to 12. The teacher then does the same guidance lesson on all three days with three different groups. By the end of the week the entire homeroom has experienced the lesson topic. The small-group arrangement encourages interaction and dialogue among students in the groups.

The counselors teach a guidance lesson in every classroom once every four weeks. They also provide teachers with ideas and activities that can be used for the next four small group lessons. The guidance curriculum provides goals and objectives for each grade level (6 to 8). Teachers can also develop their own activities based on team and student needs. Usually all the teachers in one team teach the same activity each week.

The school is divided into two schools—A and B. Each school has an equal number of sixth, seventh, and eighth grade classes. This arrangement reflects a school-within-a-school concept. Teams consist of two to three teachers and 60 to 90 students for all academic classes, homerooms, and advisement. Teams of teachers have common planning periods. Common planning enables the teams to discuss the progress of individual students and to generate topics for small group advisement.

Advisement is integral to the student-centered total school program. It is through advisement that the guidance curriculum is offered at each grade level. The curriculum complements the total school curriculum and includes educational, career, and personal/social topics. Teacher-advisers augment the guidance curriculum with other activities that include school orientation, sustained silent reading, journal writing, community help projects, current events, and small-group family albums. The focus is on developing a sense of community.

Individual conferences between advisees and advisers are an outgrowth of the small-group sessions. As both the homeroom teacher and academic teacher, the teacher advisers get to know their students very well. Thus, they are in a position to provide individual assistance and to refer students to the counselor when necessary. Teacher offices are located adjacent to their classrooms, facilitating individual conferences. Advisers also keep in close touch with parents. At the end of the sixth and seventh grade years, the advisers on each team discuss each advisee and recommend placement for the following year.

The school offers a traditional seven-period schedule with physical education scheduled four times per week for each student. On the fifth day, the students are scheduled into small-group guidance with their advisers. Advisers meet with a third of their homeroom students on Tuesdays, another third on Wednesdays, and the last third on Thursdays. A student with small group on Tuesday is scheduled for physical education on Monday, Wednesday, Thursday, and Friday all year. The seven-period day allows teacher-advisers to have double planning on Mondays and Fridays and single-period planning on Tuesday, Wednesday, and Thursday.

Wakulla Middle School offers a somewhat different approach to advisement that brings the classroom teachers and the counselors together on behalf of the students. The closeness of this relationship enables advisers to refer students easily to counselors for special help and to consult with counselors to receive help in carrying out their responsibilities.

COMMON THREADS

Although each program described in this chapter is different, they all have several commonalities. Each school has had advisement programs for many years. New Trier began in 1924. Bishop Carroll's program began when the school opened in 1971. Freedom High School and McCleur North also date back to 1971. Shoreham-Wading River instituted its program in 1972, when the school was planned. The long-term commitment to the program in these schools seems obvious

The strength of these different approaches to advisement and advocacy is in the close relationships between advisers and advisees and advisers and professional counselors. The schools' goal is to provide a successful educational experience for each student. Identifying one adult-professional as a student's adviser gives each student someone at the school to whom the student can turn for help.

Obviously, all teacher-advisers are not equal, just as all teachers are not equal. The key, however, is to have all advisers meet minimal responsibilities and to allow others to exceed them. All of the schools find time during the day for teachers to meet these responsibilities. On average, advisement appears to require about five hours of an adviser's time each week. It seems much easier for a teacher to say yes to advisement responsibilities when "company" time is provided.

And finally, principals in the featured schools not only find time for teachers to advise and for advisees to meet with their advisees, they often serve as advisers themselves, and provide resources in the form of people, materials, and staff development.

4

ORGANIZING A SCHOOL ADVISEMENT SYSTEM

THE CLUSTER ARRANGEMENT

Just as an advisement system aims to personalize the education process, the structure of the system supports that personal touch, shrinking the school to manageable groupings. It is important to consider the primary purposes of the advisement system in designing the overall advisement structure and later in structuring the individual groups.

- ◆ Is the primary purpose the improvement of communication within the building; that is, ensuring that all important information gets to every student via a concerned adult?

- ◆ Is the primary purpose extending the functions of the guidance office; that is, distributing testing information, college, and scholarship information, assessing career possibilities, or addressing common teenage issues, such as depression, substance abuse, and drinking?

- ◆ Is the primary purpose instruction, that is, orienting ninth graders to the study demands of high school, teaching testing skills to eleventh graders in preparation for SATs and ACT, or monitoring seniors through the college application process?

- ◆ Is the primary purpose academic advisement and monitoring of academic performance?

♦ Or are all these purposes, and others, part of the advisement vision?

Before settling on a structure, staff must seriously discuss the outcomes they desire.

With the defining of outcomes, structure follows naturally. Generally, the overall structure is defined by some form of clustering of adviser groups to enhance the achievement of outcomes. Here are several possibilities.

GRADE-LEVEL CLUSTERS

An obvious example, clustering adviser groups by grade level is simple and, in the case of a tentative commitment by staff, capitalizes on a familiar structure in many schools—homerooms. Students are assigned to adviser groups according to grade level, ninth-grade adviser groups, for example; and advisers may stay at the same level, receiving a new group of students each year, or move with students through grades 10 to 12, returning to ninth grade four years later. Whether assignment of students within a grade level is alphabetical, random, or by some other design depends, again, on the desired outcomes. If an outcome is for students to develop a better understanding of the diverse populations within a school, then the person responsible for creating the groups might make decisions about members of the group based on gender, race, and ethnicity. If a population is essentially homogeneous, other factors might drive the decisions about individual assignment. Whether advisers stay with a group for several years or receive a new group each year is again a decision driven by the desired outcomes. Clearly, stronger adviser-advisee relationships develop in a multiyear assignment. The question is whether that stronger relationship is critical to achieving the outcomes of the advisement program.

STRENGTHS

♦ Provides an easy assignment process.

Students in each grade level are simply divided into groups and assigned a teacher-adviser, usually one who also teaches that level.

♦ Facilitates communication of grade-specific information such as SAT/ACT information or the college application process.

♦ Facilitates, in a monitored environment, the interactions of students at one grade level.

This arrangement serves very well as a vehicle for level-specific interpersonal activities, for example, activities that help students get to know each other as in the case of sixth or ninth graders; or activities that help students deal with a particular human relations problem as in the case of ninth graders handling hazing by upperclass students.

♦ Develops strong grade-specific skills in advisers if advisers stay connected to one level.

A ninth-grade adviser becomes extremely skilled in evaluating a ninth-grader's study skills and coaching him to better skills. A sophomore adviser develops real insight into the tendency of tenth graders to let down academically and intervenes before there is serious damage. An adviser of eleventh graders is on top of the career options for an advisee and engages the student in thoughtful conversation about and planning for significant decisions that are on the horizon. The twelfth-grade adviser "rides herd" on seniors, making sure that they are working on essays, meeting application deadlines, and staying abreast of cap and gown and graduation invitation orders. Each grade level has very specific needs, and a real strength of grade-level advisers is that they become experts in the needs of that group.

Drawbacks

♦ Inhibits global view of advisement if advisers stay connected to one level.

This issue is parallel to the isolation that can develop for a teacher who instructs at one level for many years; for example, the English teacher who teaches only ninth graders for many years can lose sight of the standards a senior composition must meet and, totally unaware, slip in his or her expectations for the writing of ninth graders. Similarly, being anchored in one grade level, an adviser may become too narrow, losing (or never fully developing) a global view of advisement and thus not providing the best guidance to students for their long-term growth.

♦ Inhibits broad base of knowledge if advisers stay connected to one level.

A grade-level adviser inevitably has less knowledge of the topics beyond the needs of his or her advisees. A ninth-grade adviser may have minimal knowledge of the SATs, or a twelfth-grade adviser may not fully comprehend the work that needs to be done with ninth graders related to organizational and study skills. In the information-overloaded educational world, most educators restrict themselves to "must know" information.

♦ Restricts cross-grade interactions thus limiting the access of younger students to positive upper-level role models.

Students certainly sometimes find their role models within their age group, but it is much more likely that they will look to older groups for their role models. Grade-level adviser groups restrict this possibility.

♦ Requires ongoing articulation between levels.

Whether the model is a new adviser each year or an adviser moving with a group for four years, there must be ongoing articulation from level to level. In the former case, the present adviser must provide the next adviser with background and materials on each advisee; in the latter, the adviser must receive training in the necessary knowledge and skills for each grade level.

CROSS-GRADE CLUSTERS

Cross-grade clusters, as the term indicates, cross grades. In a grades 9 to 12 high school, for example, every adviser group contains students from all four levels. A primary goal of this arrangement is the interaction of students of various ages; under the supervision of a responsible adult, the younger students gain maturation and the older students develop empathy through their regular association with each other. Students may be assigned in a random fashion or in a more controlled fashion, as described in Grade-Level Clusters, but the first objective is to get a good mix of students by age. In this model, advisers usually keep advisees for their full high school experience, receiving them as freshmen and advising them until graduation.

STRENGTHS

♦ Facilitates, under adult supervision, interactions between younger and older students.

The creation of a school "community" is one of the major goals of an advisement program. In the same way that family members have to learn to operate as a family, a school has to learn how to operate as a community. An adviser has a unique opportunity to assist advisees in learning how to operate as a community, how to treat each other, be supportive of each other, respect each other. Older advisees can have a wonderful calming effect on rambunctious younger group members, while the enthusiasm of younger advisees can stimulate the older ones. Immature older advisees can learn a great deal through interactions with mature younger advisees, and older advisees who are further along in their course work can be exceptional tutors.

♦ Exposes younger students to positive, older-student role models.

For many students the only regular exposure to a positive role model is through participation in extracurricular activities, such as sports, marching band, the spring musical, and the like. But every student cannot be part of an extracurricular activity. A cross-grade adviser group gives students a regular opportunity to interact with an older student who is functioning well in the school community.

♦ Develops broad-based advisement skills in advisers.

Cross-grade advisement allows advisers to hone their skills by providing advisers with *ongoing experiences* in, for example, ninth-grade socialization, the notorious tenth-grade academic slump, eleventh-grade overcommitment, and twelfth-grade college jitters.

♦ Expands the adviser's in-depth knowledge of individual advisees.

Over a period of three years in a middle school or four years in a high school, an adviser accumulates a treasure trove of information about an advisee:

- How to approach the student with good news or bad news; what the student's academic strengths and weaknesses are;

- What the student's family is like and whether the student's parents/guardians are active or passive in the student's life;

- Who the student's friends are and how susceptible the student is to their pressure;

- What the student's hopes and dreams are; and

- What the student's personal fears and weaknesses are.

Having this kind of knowledge makes the adviser a treasured figure in the advisee's academic decisions.

DRAWBACKS

♦ Results in a longer assignment process as more time is required to create a balance of students from each grade level in each adviser group.

♦ Exposes younger students to possible negative influence of older students.

Ideally, students would be exposed to no negative influences. But realistically, they are. Having a concerned adult close at hand to offset or monitor the degree of negative influence can help a young advisee learn to cope with such an issue in a problem solving way.

♦ Requires adviser to be conversant with a broader range of knowledge.

The adviser must be knowledgeable about

- The full range of academic issues from adjustment to high school instruction to preparation for college testing to decisions about post-high-school life;

- The full range of maturational issues from making the transition from elementary school to middle school to consideration of how many extra-curricular activities to attempt in ninth grade; and

- The full range of social issues from coping with being cut from a junior varsity team to not being invited to the Homecoming Dance to coping with peer pressure to experiment with drugs and sex.

COMBINED GRADE-LEVEL, CROSS-GRADE CLUSTERS

This model attempts to capture the advantages of two designs, usually operating both as a pure Grade-Level Cluster, often in grades 6 or 9, *and* as a Cross-Grade Cluster in grades 7 to 8 or 10 to 12. The primary goals of this arrangement are to provide specific attention to the needs of students in "transition," from elementary to middle school or middle to high school, and to capitalize on the pluses of mixed-age grouping. The strengths and drawbacks are as indicated earlier for grade-level and cross-grade clusters with the following additions.

STRENGTHS

♦ Captures the best points of two cluster arrangements, in particular, allowing the pure-grade groups to focus fully on academic and social issues unique to those students before providing interactions with older students. For example, sixth or ninth graders are provided orientation, stability, and security at a vulnerable transition point and then move to broader, more challenging interactions.

DRAWBACKS

♦ Presents the drawbacks of two cluster models.

♦ Wears, over time, on the advisers in the transition grade, by keeping their view of advisement narrow and limiting their opportunity to experience the pleasure of seeing advisees develop into young adults who can successfully manage their own lives

ADVISER-COUNSELOR-ADMINISTRATOR CLUSTERS

This way of organizing adviser groups begins with one of the formats already described. But it goes a step further in order to enhance and facilitate consistent communication. This arrangement "clusters" a group of advisers with a counselor (as described in Chapter 3) and, ideally, with an administrator as well (see Figure 4.1). The advisers in a cluster work with this same counselor and administrator for all advisee needs—academic, emotional, social, and disciplinary. Advisees and their parents know who their counselor and administrator are and feel free to approach either as they do the adviser.

Figure 4.1. A Sample Advisement Organization for a High School of 1000 Students

Administrator 1
Counselor 1
12–15 Advisers
300–350 Students

Administrator 2
Counselor 2
12–15 Advisers
300–350 Students

Administrator 3
Counselor 3
12–15 Advisers
300–350 Students

Clusters can be determined in any way already described. But often, in the interest of improving communication, the counselors select advisers with whom they have some rapport and the advisees select an adviser with whom they have some rapport. If the cluster administrator is assigned in the same way, consistent communication is almost ensured, and the likelihood of individual advocacy increases greatly. The cluster adults meet regularly to discuss topics or issues common to the group or to prepare an activity that all adviser groups will do. For example, advisers at Wilde Lake High School in Columbia, Maryland, meet in early November to receive information from the counselors on risk factors for student suicide; this information is reviewed and discussed at this time because suicides are more prevalent during a holiday season. At this school, adviser-counselor-administrator clusters also meet to discuss any schoolwide problem, concern, or need, and to develop a related activity to be done with all advisees in a group meeting.

The adviser-counselor-administrator cluster provides a way of further personalizing the education process. Breaking the school into smaller cohesive units, each of which is managed by a group of collaborative adults, creates small "communities" with many of the advantages that small communities have— shared knowledge, the ability to act more quickly, a sense of belonging, a common focus, common goals. The bonds between the individual adviser and advisee are reinforced in this model by the additional bonds that develop between advisers and counselor, between advisers and administrator, and between counselor and administrator. These layers of collaboration increase the benefits to students exponentially.

STRENGTHS

- Enhances consistent, ongoing communication.
- Capitalizes on the cohesion of congenial grouping.
- Broadens the knowledge and involvement of key adults, thus enhancing student advocacy.
- Provides students, teacher advisers, counselors, and administrators with choices in interpersonal relationships.

DRAWBACKS

- Complicates the assignment process because allowing choices for students and adults adds another factor to be considered in determining advisory group and cluster make-up.

ASSIGNING STUDENTS TO ADVISERS

This process has been touched on earlier in the section on clusters. At its simplest, advisee assignment is the alphabetic division of students among advisers. At its most complex, the assignment process allows students to select an adviser. Cluster arrangement will in some degree dictate the advisee assignment process. Several alternatives follow, in order of increasing complexity.

- *Alphabetical*—the assignment of students to advisers by dividing up an alphabetical list. This process can be straight alphabetical from a list of all students, or it can be manipulated somewhat by working from two alphabetical lists—one female, one male.
- *Random*—the assignment of students to advisers by any random procedure. This process could be pure random, or controlled random, which might assign every 25th student to adviser A. Either way, a computer simplifies the process.

- *Selective*—the assignment of students to advisers according to a set of criteria, such as age, gender, ethnicity, race. This process requires a human hand but is very effective in producing truly diverse groups.

- *Student-Adviser Choice*—the assignment of students to advisers through a system of choices, in which both the adviser and advisee have input. In this process, advisees make several choices of desired advisors and are guaranteed one of the top three, perhaps. The adviser has an opportunity to look at a proposed list and to exercise a veto. A clerical staff member, a counselor, an adviser coordinator, or a group of interested teachers can administer the assignment process. Administrative input is essential. It is important to reinforce the importance of program outcomes in selecting a method of advisee assignment. The strongest advisement program will result when the assignment process closely aligns with outcomes.

THE RELATIONSHIP OF ADVISEMENT TO COUNSELING

The question of the relationship of advisement to counseling is a common one. Advisement does not replace counseling, but it does extend some aspects of counseling, particularly regular individual contact and the readily available listener. Listening well is perhaps the most critical skill of an adviser. Careful listening enables the adviser to know when to refer an advisee problem to the professionally trained counselor, and it is essential for an adviser to recognize when a problem is beyond her/his skill. The following is a list of the responsibilities that clearly fall to each role. Regular communication between advisers and the cluster counselor and cluster administrator can help clarify any problem that seems to fall in a gray area. The rule of thumb for the adviser must always be to seek the advice of the counselor (or the administrator) in any questionable situation.

ADVISER RESPONSIBILITIES

- ◆ Academic advisement

  This is the realm of course selection, credits, interim reports, and report cards. The adviser can keep this information in a notebook with a section for each advisee, in a separate file folder for each advisee, or in a computer database. The information serves as a basis for conferences and allows the adviser to be the most knowledgeable person in the school about the advisee's goals and performance.

- ◆ Attendance

  If the adviser meets students at the beginning of the school day, then the keeping of an attendance record is a critical responsibility as this record is the legal documentation of the student's days present and absent. If this responsibility is not the adviser's, the adviser will still want to monitor student attendance through the daily attendance bulletins as attendance has a major impact on academic performance. The adviser may keep this information in a variety of ways depending on school expectations and personal preference. A student's attendance record is often a good reason for a call to a parent.

- ◆ Communication with teachers

  The adviser will find it a regular need to speak to colleagues about an advisee, checking on attendance, performance, or behavior problems. It is helpful if a staff that is just beginning an advisement program predetermines the parameters of such interactions. To facilitate the process, teachers who are unused to dealing with each other regarding students issues may need training in how to address and resolve advisee issues in nonthreatening ways.

- ◆ Study techniques

  The mastery of study skills and techniques is of critical importance at all levels of learning. Students who gain these skills early in their school careers have a clear advantage over their peers. Chances are the adviser will need to individualize this assistance to advisees. High-performing students need only an occasional suggestion, usually related to an encounter with a new subject, but some advisees need extensive support with organization of their materials, studying for tests, or adjusting to a teacher's style. Particularly at the high school level where performance is becoming an increasingly high-stakes issue in the public schools, the advisee can profit from an adviser's guidance and monitoring.

♦ Time management

Many students at the middle and high school levels need help with time management. As young people gradually assume more responsibility for decisions about how they will spend their out-of-school time, they must grapple with balancing schoolwork and other activities. An adviser can help students look at how they spend their time and help them learn how to determine how much they can handle and how to make adjustments in a busy schedule.

♦ Minor advisee problems with staff, other students, parents, self

There probably does not exist a preteen or a teenager who does not have an occasional interpersonal or internal conflict—a conviction that a teacher hates him, anger over someone gossiping about her, an argument with a parent over curfew, stress over being accepted in an admired group of youngsters. While the conflict may truly be minor in the larger scheme of life, it is of critical importance to the young person. The adviser plays a very useful role as listener and helper in solving everyday problems. Simply helping a teen walk through how the teen might handle a situation is a significant instructional experience. As the advisee's advocate, the adviser is in a unique and valuable position to help the advisee develop problem-solving skills without seeming to interfere or coerce.

♦ Record of the advisee's information

Part of this task is the keeping of the information relating to academic performance, discussed earlier. But it also is the keeping of another significant aspect of the advisee's life at the high school level—the young person's high school history. This information includes a yearly record of extracurricular activities, community involvement, employment, awards and recognition, career interests, and so forth. As the adviser collects and updates this information, the adviser becomes increasingly knowledgeable about the advisee as a person and is in a more informed position to guide the advisee through the many choices to be made in high school. Obviously, the adviser is the person best able to write any kind of recommendation for the advisee. And most important of all, the regular attention to this information teaches the advisee the importance of keeping such a bank of readily accessible information for use in resumes, essays and applications.

COUNSELOR RESPONSIBILITIES

♦ Abuse/neglect

Any kind of abuse or neglect, suspected or substantiated, is out of the realm of adviser responsibility except for reporting it. The adviser often *stumbles* on these situations as in the case of an adviser who, in questioning a 15-year-old girl about facial and arm bruises, discovered that an older brother was battering her because he disapproved of her increasingly American appearance and behavior; in this family's culture, such behavior by an older brother was allowable. The counselor is the appropriate person to pursue matters relating to abuse/neglect, to provide or find support services for a student, and to monitor a situation in conjunction with social services and/or the police.

♦ Change of teacher or adviser

If there is a need for a change of adviser or teacher, the counselor is the appropriate person to handle the matter to preserve confidentiality and a professional atmosphere among staff. To work together effectively and to support each other in an advisement program, teacher-advisers need to feel comfortable that their peers are not discussing them in personal ways with students.

♦ Drug and/or alcohol problems

An adviser who suspects that an advisee has a drug or alcohol problem must refer this advisee to a counselor. The counselor is trained to probe such problems in a professional way, to recognize warning signs, and to approach parents in a nonthreatening way.

♦ Educational or vocational planning

Although an adviser serves very well as a general counselor and sounding board for an advisee's educational or vocational aspirations, the counselor is the correct person to provide in-depth advice. Counselors have detailed information about the various kinds of aptitude and other tests as well as interest inventories. They can provide the advisee with technical assistance in the use of computer programs and online resources. They are knowledgeable about the strengths and drawbacks of a variety of colleges, universities, and technical schools. They simply have a level of expertise that the adviser does not have.

♦ Family problems

An adviser can certainly listen to a distraught, angry, or confused parent. But helping that parent solve or find help to solve serious problems is, again, a job for a counselor. The counselor's training and knowledge of school system and community resources for families make the counselor the appropriate resource. An adviser simply does not have the time or the training to assume responsibility for such problems.

♦ Legal problems, such as guardianship or probation

Although the counselor is not the person who will resolve these kinds of problems, the counselor can pursue with the administration both information and resolution.

♦ Personal problems that border on crisis

Most teacher-advisers would know to take severe problems, such as an advisee's threat to run away or to commit suicide, to a counselor. The important factor is that the problem be taken to the counselor *immediately*.

♦ Pregnancy

The many issues surrounding pregnancy—from decisions about the pregnancy to prenatal care to financial issues—require the involvement of skilled personnel. The counselor is the appropriate person to counsel a pregnant teen and to connect her and her family to necessary resources.

♦ Referral to community agencies

One of the jobs of guidance counselors is to maintain a databank of community agencies and to become knowledgeable about the resources of each agency. Although an adviser may have knowledge about a few agencies, the counselor is the person to make referrals or to give that task to a school psychologist or other appropriate employee.

♦ Runaways

Advisers are often the first person to know that a student is a runaway. This information must go to guidance and the administration who will then work with the police on any matters that involve the school.

♦ Severe academic problems

An adviser should refer to guidance any student whose academic problems go beyond the typical failure to do homework or study for a test. A student who seems unable to do anything, who is unwilling to do anything, who appears to be doing all the right things but still performs poorly, who has a serious cheating problem—such students need the attention of a counselor. These surface behaviors typically cover complicated under-the-surface problems.

♦ Students who are overly withdrawn or overly aggressive

These students are obvious candidates for a counselor's help. The adviser is highly likely to refer the overly aggressive advisee for help but, not wanting to be intrusive, may overlook the withdrawn advisee. An advisee who does not bond with an adviser and seeks no change of advisers is a good candidate for referral to a counselor.

♦ Test scores, aptitudes, learning problems

Because another area of extensive counselor training is the area of testing and aptitude, the counselor is the most knowledgeable person about these topics.

(The foregoing unannotated lists are drawn from Keefe (1983) and Advisory Task Force (1987).)

The division of responsibilities between advisers and counselors turns on several factors: how serious is the problem; who has the appropriate training; who has the most experience; who has the time. There is plenty of work for both adviser and counselor. Sharing the work makes each load more manageable and ensures the most personal, most knowledgeable support for each advisee.

WHO SHOULD ADVISE?

The answer to this question depends on the desired outcomes of the advisement program. It is possible for every staff member in a school—from teacher to administrator to instructional assistant to custodian—to serve as an adviser. At River Hill High School in Clarksville, Maryland, the principal and several of the counselors serve as advisers. The plus of such an expectation is that advisement is seen as a critical role for every adult and as essential to the school program. The minus is that during adviser time, no one may be readily available to provide special services, such as instruction in the college application process, or emergency services, such as dealing with a stopped up commode! Reality and practicality thus dictate some restrictions on who should advise. One rule must apply: all eligible staff members participate. Contrary to what might be believed, every teacher *is* capable of serving as an adviser, and even if students have the option of choice, no teacher will ever *not* be selected. Some advisers might have a reduced advisee load because of other demanding responsibilities; for example, a principal, an assistant principal, the student government adviser, or the athletic director; or these individuals might be paired with a new adviser in an apprenticeship arrangement, thus giving the experienced person some flexibility in balancing the adviser responsibilities and other responsibilities. *For the health of the advisement program, every eligible person must be an active participant.*

ADMINISTERING A PROGRAM

Key to the success of any advisement system is a clear delineation of guidelines and responsibilities. No two programs are likely to operate the same way, but there are some common administrative questions to be posed and answered. All staff who are to be involved in the program should participate in answering the following questions, and it would be wise to involve students and parents in reviewing the design.

   ◆ Who will design the program? Who will develop the yearly schedule and the activities? How many group meetings will occur each week, when, and where? What will be the expectations for individual conferences, for record keeping, for parent contacts? Who will monitor the implementation of the program?

♦ How many persons are needed to provide a reasonable adviser-advisee load? As is true in the classroom, the number of advisees is a critical concern in ensuring good advisement. Twenty is an absolute maximum; 10 would be better. The number for effective advisement, however, is less dependent on number than on the *time provided* for the adviser to meet expectations.

♦ How much training is necessary? Who is available to provide it *and* to provide support once the program is under way? Will the training be ongoing? How will new advisers be trained, once the program is in place? (See Chapter 6.)

♦ If advisement is to be an extension of guidance, will counselors be available to assist advisers in implementing certain activities, such as group discussions? What will be the referral process to counselors for problems that go beyond the adviser's expertise or responsibility? How will the counselor provide feedback to the adviser?

♦ Who will monitor the operations of adviser groups? Someone must be responsible for the advisement program. Will this be an administrator, the administrative team, a designated teacher or group of teachers, a counselor? If anyone other than an administrator, will that individual or group have additional time built into the day to oversee the program?

♦ What will be the evaluation system? Who will design it? Administer it? Interpret the data? What kinds of quantitative and qualitative data will be collected? Who will make the decisions about data-driven adjustments in the program—the administration, a school improvement team, an advisement committee?

SCHEDULING TIME TO ADVISE

Aside from selling the concept of advisement to teachers, the issue of time is the most difficult of the problems relating to advisement in public schools. In the public school world that increasingly sees little room for anything beyond testing and preparation for testing, setting aside time for advisement may be a truly difficult hurdle. Yet advisement, particularly academic advisement, is more important than it has ever been to the attainment of a meaningful high school diploma. To be an effective adviser requires about five hours per week; those hours are spent conferring with advisees; communicating with parents, teachers, counselors, and administrators; maintaining records; and participating in sessions to strengthen adviser skills. In traditional and modular schedules, an adviser needs one period or two modules per day to accomplish adviser tasks. In a 90-minute-block schedule, each adviser needs three blocks a week. In a nontraditional schedule (see quality exemplars *Bishop Carroll* (p. 36) and *Thomas Haney* (p. 50) in Chapter 3), advisory time flexes to meet the needs of individual students and the outcomes of the program.

Clearly, built-in advisory time is necessary if an advisement system is to be viable. The challenge becomes how to carve advisement time out of a school day that is increasingly packed. For schools in traditional, modular, and block schedules, there are essentially two options to consider.

- ◆ One-on-one advisement

    This is the ideal but also the most difficult way in most public school schedules. Given that students now leave scheduled classes to participate in a music sectional or to work with a counselor, college representative, or speech pathologist, it is not unreasonable to think in terms of having a student leave a class briefly for an individual conference with an adviser. This is actually the easy part. The hard part is figuring out how to provide the teacher-adviser with that amount of time. Some teachers would be willingly to occasionally give up part of a planning period to meet with an advisee; others would find such an expectation unacceptable. Many high schools, particularly those operating block schedules, provide a break during the morning. It is possible to expand that break to include advisory time, using some days for group meetings and some days for prescheduled, individual appointments. Before- or after-school conferences are certainly a possibility; dependent, of course, on the whimsical memories of students!

♦ Group advisement

Creating an adviser period of 20 to 25 minutes to occur on a regular basis is the second common method of providing advisory time. This plan ensures adviser-advisee contact, but it makes private conferring a challenge unless a teacher has a very large room. Part of the period could be used for general advisement or for a group activity, and the remainder for one or two individual conferences. There is always a concern about "down time" for the students not being advised, but advisees can plan to do homework or make an appointment to see a counselor or visit with a college/vocational school representative or even go to the cafeteria for a snack.

The positive academic and behavioral results of a strong advisement program support the investment of time to do the job right. Schools that commit time to advisement provide a meaningful personal relationship for every student, guaranteeing that each one is known well by at least one adult in the building.

Appendix E offers examples of master schedules for middle and high schools that incorporate advisement. Finding time for teachers to advise, however, remains problematic. Most secondary school teachers are assigned the equivalent of five periods of teaching in a six-period day. Implementing an advisement program in this setting is difficult, but not impossible. Teachers must be convinced that be adding advisement to their daily teaching assignment is both personally and collectively beneficial. In William Glasser's terms, they must see advisement as adding a measure of quality to their lives. This can be achieved, at least partially, by exposing them to motivational speakers or visiting schools with successful advisement programs or viewing poignant films, such as "Cipher in the Snow." It also helps if the principal and other nonteaching professionals serve as advisers.

Several approaches to school organization can facilitate the implementation of an advisement program. Variations of the following schemes are in place in secondary schools implementing advisement:

♦ The seven-period day often provides two planning periods for teachers. Teachers teach five, have a planning period, and do advisement the other period. This arrangement does not address the overload question nor does it facilitate individual conferences with students unless teachers are willing to release students from class.

♦ One form of block scheduling, more frequently found at the middle level, assigns a finite number of students to a team of teachers. The team schedules students into academic subjects based on student need and teacher competence. For example, a four-hour block of time can be divided into periods of language arts, mathematics, science, and social studies or it can be divided in anyway the teaching team desires. The team can assign students to teacher-advisers within the team who can meet individually with them or in groups as necessary. This approach has the added benefit of the team of teachers also serving as the students' academic teachers, giving them an opportunity to know their advisees quite well and to focus their one-to-one conferences on academic progress.

♦ Schools implementing a continuous progress or performance-based instructional program provide more flexible schedules for teachers and students. Teachers are scheduled with students fewer hours each day as students work independently or in learning teams. A typical teacher schedule might involve supervising students as they work on learning guides two or three hours per day, planning one or two hours per day, and meeting with advisees one hour per day. In the NASSP Models Schools Project (1969-74), teachers were scheduled for direct contact with students in an academic setting 25 hours every 2 weeks. The remainder of their time was devoted to developing instructional materials, planning, and advisement.

Successful advisement programs are given priority by school personnel because they see the benefits they provide for all school stakeholders. The way to implement a program at a school level is best determined by the school staff. Schools are systems that either support or inhibit successful implementations. Simply adding advisement to teachers' and students' schedules often disrupts because it fails to acknowledge that changes in one part of a system invariably affect all parts of the system.

5

EXPECTATIONS AND ADVISEMENT: WHAT ADVISERS DO

A good adviser does a lot! The role as a student advocate is part academic monitor, part counselor, part friend, part parent, part communicator, part mediator, part facilitator. All teachers have these skills, although some claim they do not. Every teacher daily develops these skills in interactions with students, staff, and parents. Advisement hones these skills as advisers focus on the specific strengths and weaknesses of a small group of students that they come to know very well.

KNOWING STUDENTS WELL

There is an incisive maxim hanging on the wall of a ninth-grade social studies classroom at Wilde Lake High School in Columbia, Maryland: "They won't care how much you know until they know how much you care." Whether or not things should work this way in schools, they often do work this way for many students. William Glasser first addressed this phenomenon in *The Identity Society* (1972) and elaborated its academic implications in *The Quality School* (1990). Students keep school and the adults in it as part of their "quality world" when they perceive school as good for them. In the role of significant school adult, the teacher-adviser aims to be part of that quality world, to know the student well, and to function as an advocate for the student in every arena. A boost to this adviser-advisee link is to allow advisers and advisees to have a voice in the selection process (see Chapter 4); doing so establishes an immediate personal bond—"I like you"—and ensures that a communication link is easier to establish. But the adviser needs to take other steps to get to know an advisee better.

Having advisees complete interest inventories provides helpful background information. What subjects does the advisee like most? What extracurricular activities does the advisee participate in? What does the advisee like to do in his or her spare time? Having advisees provide noninvasive information about family members helps clarify family relationships. How many siblings does the advisee have, and where is the advisee in the lineup? Do other family members live close by? Do grandparents live in the home? Asking for information about outside responsibilities or jobs or commitments can be enlightening with regard to academic performance. How many hours does the advisee work each week? Is the advisee active in church groups or community groups? (See Appendix A.)

Discussing with an advisee his or her learning style and coping strategies can provide invaluable data for the adviser and the advisee. Some schools require students to carry a learning style profile in their notebooks in an effort to increase students' awareness of how a learning environment fits them—or does not. (See Chapter 6.)

BECOMING A FRIEND

People tend to accept advice from a friend more readily than from a relative stranger. Thus, it follows that an advisee will more readily accept advice from an adviser who is perceived as a friend. Being friendly means greeting an advisee warmly, congratulating him or her on a success, cheering him or her up when she or he is discouraged, consoling her when there is a disappointment or tragedy, simply treating the young person as a special person worth knowing. There are many things that advisers and advisees can do together to build a friendly relationship: attend school athletic events, participate in competitions between advisory groups, plan advisory breakfasts, attend plays or visit museums, have an end-of-year picnic.

But this topic of friendship brings a caution. Just as a teacher's becoming a friend to a student creates the risk of either the student or the teacher misunderstanding the line that still exists between the two, so an adviser's becoming a friend to an advisee creates the same risk. All of the cautions that are put forth regarding teacher-student friendships apply to adviser-advisee friendships. The adviser is an *adult* friend, ideally a role model, and thus is an appropriate ear for hopes and dreams, as well as for frustrations and disappointments regarding school, teachers, or parents. Advisees often use an adviser in this manner. Like a friend, the adviser can be supportive and sympathetic. Unlike a friend, however, the adviser must not encourage criticism of, participate in criticism of, or make judgments about colleagues or parents. The adviser can suggest ways of addressing a problem, can—if the adviser has the skills—offer to mediate a problem, or can refer the student to a counselor or an administrator. The adviser, even though a friend, must remember that "friend" is a qualified word when used with an advisee; being personable and supportive does not mean being a "buddy."

FACILITATING ADVISEE INTERACTIONS

In an advisement program that incorporates group activities, the adviser plays a key role in the interplay among advisees. When Wilde Lake High School opened in 1971, one purpose of the adviser group was to help the students, who were coming from several different schools, to create a sense of school community and spirit. That role has continued over 28 years. In recent years, Wednesday was group activity day, with some group activities being optional and others being mandatory. Advisory Group Coordinator Eric Ebersole met with the counselors, the principal, and individual advisers on a regular basis to determine the kinds of activities needed. Human relations activities included icebreaking activities in the beginning of the year to help advisees get to know each other better, a scavenger hunt activity to introduce new students to and to test returning students' memories of the building and school services, and a "Decorate Your Adviser" competition to drum up school spirit and celebrate the coming winter holiday. As advisers guide advisees through activities such as these, they facilitate the development of interpersonal skills in these young people.

MONITORING ACADEMIC PROGRESS

Although the roles of friend and group facilitator are important adviser roles, the most significant role of the adviser is academic advisement. With academic expectations for high school students increasing nationwide, the significance of this role increases. The Introduction states, "When specific benchmarks for student achievement are adopted, the responsibility for helping individual students reach those plateaus falls to someone." An appropriate someone is the teacher-adviser.

For an adviser to monitor academic progress effectively, the adviser must receive the same information that the advisee does and thus must receive copies of the learning style profile (see Chapter 6), report cards, interim reports, course selection materials, and, at the high school level, college testing information and career information. An adviser also needs a regularly updated record of the advisee's credits to be knowledgeable of the advisee's progress toward graduation. These items provide immediate and meaningful data for regular conferences with an advisee. The adviser can celebrate a strong performance with a student as well as discuss with the student what is not working in a course where performance is mediocre or poor. The stage is then set for academic planning and follow-up monitoring. The adviser coaches the advisee in creating specific academic goals for a grading period and in establishing checkpoints for the review of performance and progress. When a checkpoint comes up, the adviser helps the advisee decide if he needs to make a course correction. If academic performance is slipping and there is no classroom explanation for the situation, the adviser may decide to contact a counselor or parent. Getting at underlying reasons and working with parents in sensitive personal areas is not an adviser's job, however; it is either a counselor's job or the job of a professional or agency outside the school.

In the areas of course selection, test interpretation, college tests, and career requirements, the high school adviser-counselor connection is critical. An adviser needs to be as knowledgeable about course content and course sequence as a counselor. It is important for an adviser to be able to discuss with an advisee course prerequisites, course links, such as the Algebra II link to chemistry, and logical course sequences where no sequence is established. But the counselor remains the resource for questions that require knowledge of college requirements and preferences. And the counselor is also the individual who assumes responsibility for keeping advisers informed· about PSATs, SATs, ACTs, all specialized testing, and the availability of career materials and career information sessions. The adviser feeds back into the process at this point by keeping advisees aware of the information that is available in the guidance office and by being certain that advisees schedule appointments with counselors to explore career goals and discuss the academic experiences needed to reach those goals. The adviser can also be helpful to an advisee who is completing college, technical school, or job applications and/or essays; using the personal information that the adviser and advisee have been keeping over the years, the adviser can assist the advisee and counselor in producing an application that will help the advisee move toward his educational goals.

The frequency of adviser-advisee academic conferences is best determined by the needs of the advisee. Students with academic difficulties or unclear academic and career goals obviously will need more time. It is important, however, not to shortchange the advisee who is doing well; this student benefits from other kinds of conversations that expand and extend his view of learning and of his possibilities and options. One individual conference per month per advisee is a reasonable benchmark.

The adviser then is the overall manager/coach of the academic progress of an advisee, counseling the advisee about performance and related topics and encouraging the advisee to work to her/his potential. The adviser becomes the authority on day-to-day academic expectations and concerns, acts as a connector and collaborator in areas where specialized knowledge is needed, and contacts parents when necessary.

PERSONAL PLANS FOR
STUDENT PROGRESS

Breaking Ranks: Changing an American Institution makes this recommendation in the first chapter: "Each student will have a Personal Plan for Progress to ensure that the high school takes individual needs into consideration and to allow students, within reasonable parameters, to design their own methods for learning in an effort to meet high standards" (NASSP, 1996, p. 11). Developing a plan for student progress is an essential, collaborative effort of adviser and advisee. High schools often require students to have a four-year plan; monitored by the guidance office, the plan usually consists of a list of courses to be taken over the four years. With an advisement system, this kind of planning takes on more meaning. A personal plan for student progress is both long-range and short-range. The long-range aspect addresses what an advisee ultimately hopes to achieve academically and what career paths the advisee is considering. The short-range aspect looks at yearly course selection, the advisee's academic strengths and weaknesses, study habits and learning style, extracurricular involvement, and interests. Together, the adviser and advisee map out strategies to assist the advisee not only in performing well but also in making and executing other plans that relate to the advisee's academic future. The plan serves as a ready source of information and an ongoing point of discussion, anchoring both the adviser and advisee in the most significant aspect of advisement. As stated in the Introduction, Keefe and Jenkins posit personalized learning as the direction for schools in the 21st century with teacher coaching and advisement as one of the key properties; other properties are profiling learner characteristics, creating a culture of collegiality, creating an interactive learning environment, providing flexible pacing and scheduling, and using performance assessment.

CHOOSING COURSES

An adviser serves a very important role in the course-selection process. As an individual fully knowledgeable of course content and sequence, the adviser can guide an advisee and parents in making selections and deciding when to take courses.

The adviser knows whether there are particular considerations regarding certain courses, has an in-house grasp of the advisee's capabilities and readiness, and knows how to advocate for the advisee. The adviser also plays an invaluable role if adjustments need to be made to the advisee's schedule. In a traditional school, the adviser can speak to involved teachers to determine what may need to be done and can then facilitate changes that are needed. In more innovative programs, advisers build student schedules, approve independent projects, and monitor community service. (See quality exemplars *Bishop Carroll* (p. 36) and *Thomas Haney* (p. 50) in Chapter 3.)

CONTACTS WITH FACULTY AND ADMINISTRATION

One of the most critical communication links in a school with an advisement system is the faculty link. Good communication always exists between some faculty members but does not necessarily exist across faculties. Thus, it is important to establish early the expectation for interactions between faculty in the adviser role and faculty in the teaching role. It is important to establish the necessity of adviser and teacher discussing a student—his strengths, interests, learning style, behavior, home obligations. Issues of turf and technique do arise, so faculty profit by receiving training in how to talk to each other in nonintimidating ways about the sensitive issues of classroom procedure and strategies for reaching students. In a school where each student carries a learning style profile, the groundwork is laid for the adviser and teacher to discuss what instructional strategies are most effective for an advisee.

The adviser-administrator link is actually easier to establish and maintain than the adviser-faculty link. A natural link exists between the adviser and the administration because of the leadership role of the administration. Teachers are accustomed to using administrators as resources or as sounding boards. Because student behavior is a significant factor in academic progress, contact with the administration is critical. The adviser must receive copies of disciplinary referrals and attendance reports. As the student's advocate, it is appropriate for the adviser to be involved in discipline, to be present at hearings, to present a positive side, to help the advisee generate a plan for improvement and make a commitment to implement it. At Shoreham-Wading River Middle School (see quality exemplar p. 52), the adviser is the first line of defense for discipline problems and handles most problems, involving a counselor or an administrator only in major situations.

CONTACTS WITH PARENTS

Regular contact with parents is both an important adviser responsibility and one that results in a high return on a small investment of time. There is almost no parent/guardian who does not welcome regular contact from a school and, in fact, value that contact highly. One of the great advantages of an adviser system is that it guarantees this contact because the adviser-advisee ratio is small enough to make such contact a manageable task. While it is difficult for a teacher to contact the parents/guardians of 125 to 150 students during a year, an adviser can find time to contact the parents/guardians of 10 to 20 advisees several times a year. And because the adviser has a finger on the pulse of the advisee's total school situation, the adviser can give the parent a big-picture analysis, whereas the individual teacher who calls can speak only to one subject. The adviser can, after a parent contact, send messages to particular teachers regarding parent concerns or satisfaction, or get a message to a counselor, or a "heads up" to an administrator. As a result, everyone involved in the academic life of the student is more knowledgeable about and better able to advocate for the student.

It is wise to establish an expectation for adviser contacts with parents. For example, it might be expected that each adviser contact every parent early in the school year with an introductory, positive telephone call, postcard, or letter. Because so many schools feature a Back-to-School Night for parents early in the year, a natural positive contact is to have parents start the evening with their student's adviser. Additional contacts might occur if an advisee is absent for several days ("How is Chris? Can I help get homework?"), if there is good news to report or celebrate, or if there is a problem. One adviser calls parents routinely while she is preparing dinner each night. At the end of the year, it might be expected that the adviser make another contact, such as attaching a brief note to each advisee's report card. Even with these few contacts, most parents/guardians would be receiving more attention from the school than ever before. Adviser contacts are a powerful message: "Your child is important to us."

SOLVING SCHOOL-RELATED PROBLEMS

Problem solving is an ongoing facet of school life. Perhaps one of the most powerful learnings for an advisee is personally assuming responsibility for solving one's own school problems or for helping to solve a schoolwide problem. Development of strong problem-solving skills is especially important to high school students who will soon be on their own.

INDIVIDUAL PROBLEM-SOLVING

Whether a problem is academic, behavioral, or social, and regardless of where it originates—in the classroom or hallways, on the playing fields, or at school social events—the key to a lasting solution is the involvement of someone who not only knows and cares about a student but also has the commitment and the time to stay with the student through the process of resolution. In this process, the adviser is critical as advocate, facilitator, collaborator, and monitor. Others may be involved at certain points—an administrator, for example, when rules are broken, or a counselor, when a student has a personal conflict with another student. But it is the adviser who is the ongoing contact, the ongoing listener, the ongoing prod, the ongoing cheerleader. It is the adviser who monitors a learning contract or behavior plan, who helps the advisee assess progress or adjust a time line, and who confirms that the goals have been met.

One significant factor bears mention here: When advisees are assigned to advisers, it is important that no adviser have an overload of *problem* students. Problem solving is only as effective as the follow-through; an overloaded adviser cannot provide adequate follow-through. This is a very practical reason for keeping the adviser-advisee ratio low, no higher than 20 to 1 and preferably lower.

A REAL-LIFE PROBLEM

BACKGROUND

Leah is a high school senior who has been with her adviser for three years, having spent her freshman year with a ninth-grade adviser. She is the oldest child in a single-parent family and lives with her mother, who works sporadically, and three much younger siblings in subsidized housing. Leah is attractive, bright, and mature beyond her years. She works part-time.

Leah's freshman year was a disaster. She cut school regularly, was in several serious conflicts with other girls, was surly to teachers, and unresponsive to overtures from her adviser, teachers, counselor, and administrator. She was suspended from school several times and ended the year with poor grades, yet with most of her credits. School clearly was not part of her *quality world*.

She started her sophomore year with a different adviser with whom she did not connect, and things began to slide downhill almost immediately. Because she seemed to have some rapport with the adviser of a friend, this adviser invited her to become one of her advisees, and the administration approved the switch. The rapport grew into a strong friendship, and Leah began to improve her attendance, performance, and behavior. Her sophomore and junior years were not without incident, but the adviser worked with her, helping her make and revise academic and behavior plans, interacting with teachers, and advocating for Leah. Gradually, Leah became more cognizant of her needs, strengths, and weaknesses, and more adept at analyzing external difficulties and making plans to manage them.

PRESENT PROBLEM

Leah is almost half way through her senior year and doing well. She is hoping to attend the local community college when she graduates, provided that she can get financial assistance, and fully understands that her academic performance and conduct must be exemplary this year. She has been working closely with her counselor to complete the college application and to look for financial aid. The adviser has helped her gain a position as an office aide several periods a week to give her a stronger sense of accomplishment, and the guidance counselor has involved her in visits of selected seniors to feeder middle schools to talk to eighth graders about getting off to a good start in high school, thus giving her a chance to experience respect from younger students.

At this point, the attendance secretary sends the adviser a note indicating that Leah is suddenly compiling a string of tardies and has brought no excuses from home. Then one of Leah's teachers, meeting the adviser in the hall, mentions that Leah was unprepared for a major presentation and has thus put her strong grade in this class in jeopardy. When Leah fails to keep an appointment with the adviser, the adviser goes looking for her and finds her in the media center talking to her boyfriend, with neither of them having permission to be there. The adviser sends the boyfriend to class and begins a conversation with Leah, gently refreshing her on her personal plan and probing for the causes of Leah's sudden slip in commitment.

What Leah eventually shares is that her mother was recently arrested for public drunkenness and placed in a treatment center. Although relatives are lending a hand where they can, Leah essentially has responsibility for the younger children, for getting them to school in the morning, for preparing most of their meals, for helping them with homework at night, and for doing the laundry and other household chores. And she is continuing to report to her job, for fear of losing it if she's absent. She has not told anyone at school about the situation for fear of it being reported to social services and the younger children being removed from the home and put in foster care. The adviser comforts Leah, commending her for her care of the younger children, promises to work with her on some solutions, and takes her to class.

The adviser then contacts the counselor who connects with the school system social worker to ensure that the family unit will stay intact and that the children will receive the necessary financial support until the mother returns. The fact that Leah is already 18, that relatives are assisting, and that a social worker is now monitoring the situation is deemed a satisfactory arrangement by the authorities, and this worry is removed from Leah's shoulders.

The adviser then speaks to each of Leah's teachers, simply indicating that there is a serious family emergency and asking for temporary accommodations in expectations. She then speaks to an administrator about Leah's home responsibilities, and the administrator arranges for her lateness to be excused for the duration of the mother's absence. Meeting with Leah the next day, the adviser helps her review the problem and brainstorm the options she might have used in dealing with it.

Within a month Leah's mother is home again, and Leah's attendance and school performance return to normal. She is able to make up missed work and is soon back on track academically.

The extent of this problem-solving situation is unusual, but it is not that unusual. With so many families having only one present parent or having both parents work, today's students are often very much on their own to manage themselves and frequently siblings as well. These students profit greatly from having an adviser. But students from homes where parents are actively involved also profit from having an in-school advocate to supplement what parents do. A school advisement program is a unique safety net for young people.

SCHOOLWIDE PROBLEM SOLVING

An advisement system that incorporates regular group meetings is a ready-made vehicle for students to address a schoolwide problem. Student tardiness to school, cheating, disrespect between student groups or toward staff—these problems and many others that require some kind. As mentioned earlier, Wilde Lake High School has long used advisory groups to involve students in school needs and issues. Mandatory group activities have included one to discuss student violence toward each other (See Appendix D), one to discuss student misbehavior after a dance and to recommend expectations for future dances, one to discuss the harassment of a Muslim student, and several to discuss the challenges of a temporary move to another building.

At River Hill High School, each month is devoted to a theme, such as "Serving Others" or "Drug and Alcohol Awareness." During one group each week, advisers and advisees focus on activities related to that theme. For example, they may discuss the needs of the hungry in Maryland and make plans to collect canned food. Or they may view a video on alcohol abuse and then discuss prepared questions that get at the hard issues of teenagers' use of alcohol.

In most schools, students' experiences with the group process are inconsistent at best. Adviser group meetings with well-designed activities and skillful adviser facilitation are an ongoing experience that informally develops valuable group-process skills in advisees.

6

STAFF DEVELOPMENT

Advising students requires time, talent, commitment, and a desire to serve all students equally well. Most educators have no trouble accepting this challenge. Commitment to students was one of the reasons they chose teaching as a profession. Teaching is a helping profession, and most, if not all, educators, desire to help students and do so in varying ways within the constraints of time. The suggestions that follow reflect what we think enhances this process. The suggestions have been gleaned from the lessons of practical application in a variety of school settings. The quest to improve, however, is an individual matter. Like the students, teachers are individuals and construct their own meanings and advance by their own timetable. The content and activities described can be approached in different ways—individually, learning teams, or total faculty.

CHOICE THEORY

The basis for choice theory was broached in the section describing the satisfaction of basic needs. According to choice theory (Glasser used the term *control theory* to describe the same process), all human behavior is internally motivated and not a result of a programmed reaction to external stimuli. Individuals choose to respond or not respond in a given way. For example, the ringing of a telephone may or may not result in a person answering the phone. It is a matter of conscious choice. Because most people answer telephones when they ring, it appears logical that a ringing telephone always results in a person choosing to answer it. But anyone who has attempted to avoid speaking with unwanted callers, be they solicitors, bill collectors, or complainers, understands the individuality of the behavior. The call recipient has even more control over the process since advent of caller ID.

Students are bound by the same behavior. When they stop disrupting class or coming to school late, it isn't because the teacher or the principal has forced them to do so; it is because they see that behaving more responsibly is in their best interests. It is a choice that they have made that satisfies one of their five basic needs—survival, belonging, power, freedom, or fun. The ways in which the basic needs are fulfilled can be summarized as follows:

- ◆ Survival needs are fulfilled in a relatively straightforward fashion. If hungry one eats. If thirsty, one drinks.
- ◆ The need to belong is fulfilled by loving, sharing, and cooperating with others.
- ◆ The need for power is fulfilled by achieving, accomplishing, and being recognized and respected.
- ◆ The need for freedom is fulfilled by making choices.
- ◆ The need for fun by learning and playing. According to Glasser, fun is the genetic reward for learning.

When students fulfill their needs adequately, they experience pleasure. When they fail to fulfill their needs, they experience pain. The longer a need is frustrated; the longer the pain exists, often causing desperate attempts to fulfill the need. The abuse of drugs and alcohol, for example, are attempts to mask pain for temporary periods of time.

All humans control for the satisfaction of their basic needs. They know what they want to see, hear, and/or experience at any time. The people, places, and activities that satisfy their needs are always idiosyncratic. In the process of living, all of us have created an internal world, what Glasser calls a *quality world*, of need-fulfilling behaviors. They are analogous to the picture albums filled with snapshots of loved ones, family trips, and special events. Because their quality worlds are different, individuals behave in different ways. When students make a connection between school events and the fulfillment of one or more basic needs, they place the teacher, the subject or the activity in their quality worlds. Correspondingly, when school does not fulfill their basic needs, they withdraw it. One only has to picture the excitement of all kindergarten children coming to school on the first days to capture the power of one's quality world. Unfortunately, after several years of school as a non-need-satisfier, many of these same children begin to remove school from their quality worlds. In this context, the potential of an adviser, a teacher, or a coach for restoring the value of school for a student is unlimited.

Helping students to see the ways in which they are attempting to satisfy their needs enables them to gain a modicum of understanding of their own behavior. One way of accomplishing this end is to locate the satisfiers in a diagram similar to Figure 6.1.

FIGURE 6.1. BASIC PSYCHOLOGICAL NEEDS

Belonging	Power
Freedom	Fun

By placing a list of satisfiers under each of the needs, students can immediately assess which of the needs has few pictures, a clue as to where difficulties may exist. Then, by helping the students look into the external world to broaden their experiences they can begin to develop additional ways to meet their needs. They can gain insight into their current behavior, evaluate its effectiveness, and develop plans to decrease the gap between their aspirations and the status quo. Of course, the same things apply to teacher-advisers. They can complete the chart for themselves. In fact, an important way for teachers to become more knowledgeable about choice theory is to apply it to themselves.

As they become more comfortable with the process, teacher-advisers, in turn, can apply it to students. Several written sources are available to begin one's understanding of choice (control) theory. Four books by William Glasser—*Control Theory* (1984), *Control Theory in the Classroom* (1986), *Take Effective Control of Your Life* (1984), and *Choice Theory* (1998)—are excellent sources. Two books by Robert Wubbolding—*Changing Life for the Better* (1985) and *Using Reality Therapy* (1988)—are also helpful. Formal courses and workshops can be arranged by contacting William Glasser, M.D. Inc. 22024 Lassen Street #118, Chatsworth, CA 91311; Dr. Doug Naylor, Educator Training Center, 1891 North Gaffney Street, Suite 217, San Pedro, CA 90731; or Chelsom Consultants, 134 110th Street, Saskatoon, Saskatchewan S7N 1S2, Canada.

People who understand control theory understand that it is impossible to get someone to do what someone else wants them to do. When students understand their actions more clearly, they are in a better position to exert a measure of self-control. The late Swiss epistemologist Jean Piaget proffered that the end of education should be autonomy. Teacher-advisers working closely with students are in the advantageous position of taking a place in the student's quality world, and from that vantage point helping them take responsibility for their actions. Planning and problem solving are two social skills needed by all persons regardless of vocation. What better way to learn and extend them than in the service of one's own goals.

COGNITIVE-LEARNING STYLE

It is generally accepted by educators that students have different learning styles. They respond differently to the same learning environments. Teachers may think that they are teaching an effective lesson for all students, but, in reality, each student sees something different. Learning style is defined simply as how a student learns and how the student likes to learn. The *how of learning* reflects the level of cognitive processing. The *likes to learn* aspect of style refers to differential responses learners make to the learning environment.

There are several learning-style models available for educators. Most of the models have a method for diagnosing student style and recommending ways to adjust instruction and the learning environment to the diagnosed differences. The absence of a common paradigm for style was cited by Keefe and Ferrell (1990), indicating that many learning-style theorists have tied theory development to the development of assessment instrumentation (p. 57). The result is a narrowing of the possibilities for advancing style-based instruction beyond the various paradigms of individual theorists.

One of the most recent development in style diagnosis for secondary students is the *Learning Style Profile,* created by a task force sponsored by the National Association of Secondary Schools. The task force convened in 1982, and completed its work in 1986 with the publication of the *Profile.* The initial draft of the instrument was field-tested on 1500 students in 15 schools. The final draft was administered to a normative sample of 5000 students in over 40 different schools in the United States (Keefe & Ferrell, 1990).

The *Profile* is based upon an information-processing model of learning. It acknowledges that the business of school is to help all students acquire the knowledge and skills to succeed in the workplace. It also acknowledges that, to the degree that schools are able to provide learning environments sensitive to the learning style needs of students, the likelihood that more students will do quality work is increased (Jenkins, 1992).

The *Profile* is composed of 4 groupings, 24 independent elements of style, and 126 items. The cognitive elements form the first grouping and include analysis, spatial skill, discrimination, categorization, sequential processing, simultaneous processing, short-term visual memory, and verbal-spatial. Relative strength in each of these elements enables students to exercise greater control over the learning process. Historically, many of the cognitive elements were identified as cognitive controls to connote their power for enabling individuals to store and retrieve information effectively.

The second grouping contains three elements of perceptual response—visual, auditory, and emotive. They indicate the student's initial response to information. The scales of this section of the profile are derived from the *Edmonds Learning Style Identification Exercise* (ELSIE). Visual and auditory responses are straightforward. The emotive response is either kinesthetic or

emotional. Students who have not done well in school often develop emotional responses to specific subject matter or teachers,
or even to school in general.

The next two groupings assess students' instructional and
study preferences. They include verbal risk, persistence, manip-
ulatives, times of day, grouping, posture, mobility, sound, light-
ing, and temperature. Many of these scales are taken from the
Dunn, Dunn, and Price Learning Style Inventory, an instrument
that is widely used in grades K to 12.

The readability of the *Profile* is set at grades 5 to 6 using the
Dale-Chall Readability Formula. Students may take as long as they
wish to complete the *Profile*. Emphasis is placed on the desire to
get accurate data. Usually it takes a student between 45 and 90
minutes to complete. The cognitive elements contain right and
wrong answers. The perceptual response elements ask students
to read a list of words and record their initial first response for
each of the words. The instructional and study preferences are
measured by self-report items on a 5-point scale. The end result
is a comprehensive profile depicting a student's learning style.

Aside from the obvious value of the profile to teachers, advisers can use the profiles to give students insight into their own
learning styles and how they might adjust their own learning
environments to capitalize on their diagnosed strengths. Students tend to be very interested in information about themselves. Once they have an understanding of their styles, they can
use the information to resolve academic problems they might be
experiencing. Knowing about their individual learning style
may also be a part of improving one's intrapersonal intelligence
(see Gardner, 1983).Teacher-advisers can also talk with the
teachers of their advisees to develop strategies for improving an
advisee's academic performance. When instructional accommodations of learning style are made, students often do better academically. Students who are low in several cognitive processing
skills need special training to help them improve. Letteri (1982)
demonstrated the ability to train students to increase their facility in several cognitive skills. He found that the successful aug-
mentation of weak cognitive skills resulted in higher standardized test scores, improved grades, and improved academic performance over time.

LISTENING AS A MEANS TO STUDENT EMPOWERMENT

Listening to students is an important way to value their thoughts, opinions and ideas. When done appropriately, it helps them gain a sense of recognition and power. This is one of the reasons why the individual conference is the *sine qua non* of an advisement program. If the teacher-adviser is to be the one adult in the school who knows the advisee best, then sufficient time must be devoted to one-on-one meetings. What happens during the conferences is in control of the adviser and the advisee. When advisers really listen to what a student has to say, it establishes a bond of trust. The individual conference gives each student in the school a place in the spotlight for the duration of the conference. For many students, it becomes the only time they have a chance during a school day to be heard in a supportive environment (Jenkins, 1992).

During the individual conference, the adviser and advisee can discuss academic progress, reassess the advisee's schedule and use of time, establish goals, discuss home or school problems, or discuss aspects of the advisee's learning style and how to adjust study habits to match strengths and preferences, or they can use the time to get to know each other better.

The advisory system creates a structure in which it is acceptable for a student to talk seriously with an adult who is not a parent. As one student at Shoreham-Wading River observed, "Advisory is good. You have someone to tell your problems to." Another student remarked, "There are things you just cannot discuss with your parents. You need an adviser" (Middle School Friday Memo).

There are times when advisers meet formally with advisees' parents to discuss the advisee's academic progress, future coursework, and career plans. There are other times when parent conferences are arranged to address a specific academic or behavioral problem. In either case, the importance of hearing what the parents have to say cannot be overstated. This is especially true of parents of at-risk students who often avoid coming to school because they feel intimidated by the numbers of "educated" persons who bombard them with questions about their sons or daughters. As the advisees first line of defense, advisers are in a unique position to interpret the school to the parents and to help them feel at ease in the school environment. The message should be one of cooperation: "We can work together to provide the best educational experience for your child." Parents have the same needs as their children. Consequently, listening is important to satisfying their needs for empowerment also.

Knowing how to listen is not necessarily a skill that all teachers possess with equal facility. Assuming that counselors meet individually with teacher-advisers on a regular basis, they can model reflective listening skills. Administrators can do the same. Workshops can focus on strengthening these skills in all advisers, or they can be arranged for those advisers who need them the most. Sometimes, private organizations offer similar skills development opportunities that some teacher-advisers can attend on company time. The point to keep in mind is the importance adequate listening abilities in all advisers. How one achieves these ends can be a matter of individual programming.

UNDERSTANDING THE TOTAL SCHOOL CURRICULUM

Because advisers take an active role in monitoring the academic progress of advisees, in helping them select courses, and in developing a long-range academic plan to meet long-range goals, it is important that they have more than a cursory understanding of the total school curriculum. When a school is organized by interdisciplinary teams and students are scheduled with the teams for longer periods of time, it is more likely that teacher-advisers will have a firm grasp of a major portion of the school curriculum. Consequently, the need for specific staff development activities to inform teacher-advisers of the scope, sequence and instructional alternatives in each curricular areas would not be as great as in a more departmentalized school. They may not, however, be as informed with respect to the fine arts, the practical arts, second language, physical education, and other elective areas. Middle schools are more apt to organize by interdisciplinary teams than are high schools.

Most high schools are organized by departments. Teacher-advisers in one department are fully aware of the content and methods used in that department, but are often unfamiliar with similar arrangements in other departments. They are cognizant of the subjects, and often of the sequence in which they are recommended to be taken. What they don't know are the specific content and preferred pedagogy of each department. It seems crucial that, in working with advisees on their academic progress and course selection, the teacher-adviser have in-depth information about each department.

This information can be transmitted through written publication, on a Web site for each department, in meetings of teacher-advisers where teachers in each department present their department's curriculum and its operating procedures, or a combination of approaches. One way is to have meetings of the total faculty focus on a different department each month. Another way is to arrange for cross-departmental faculty planning areas. When teacher-advisers are well grounded in the total school curriculum, they become not only a better help-giver to their advisees but a better spokesperson for the total school.

NETWORKING WITH IN-SCHOOL and OUT-OF-SCHOOL RESOURCES

Teacher-advisers cannot resolve all issues that their advisees present. They need to know where to turn when they need help. Usually teacher-advisers are linked with professional counselors in some way. In a number of schools, the professional counselor is considered an adviser to a finite number of advisers and provides counsel and formal inservice for them. Counselors meet with advisers one-on-one on a regular basis to review their progress as advisers and respond to any problems before they get out of hand. Counselors also help advisers interpret test scores and offer specific recommendations for handling problem advisees. They develop a guidance curriculum with essential learnings for all students, usually presented in a sequence by grade levels. Aspects of the guidance curriculum are presented by the counselors, the teacher advisers, and sometimes outside speakers.

Advisers stay in touch with teachers as they monitor the progress of each advisee. They often communicate information about ways to capitalize on a particular advisee's interest or how to adjust instruction to individual student learning styles. Teachers, in turn, can offer information helpful to the adviser in conducting individual conferences with advisees or with their parents. Their insights into a student's current level of achievement can be useful in course selection and scheduling.

Teacher-advisers need to know about community resources available to individual students. This information can be provided by administrators or counselors and can be part of a teacher-advisers regular inservice. In today's ethos, knowing about where a person can turn for help with regard to drug and alcohol abuse, mental health issues, and family counseling, seems critical. Additionally, advisers need college and career information in order to respond to advisees' questions accurately. They need to know about SAT and ACT scores, and about GPAs required for admission to specific universities. They need to be able to direct advisees to programs such as Discover, so that advisees can find salient information about specific universities and specific vocations.

Advisory group activities may take advisers and advisees on camping excursions, field trips to ball games, museums, restaurants, local businesses, and community colleges, as experiences to extend their knowledge, as well as to engender a sense of belonging among the students in the advisory group. The spirit that frequently develops from such activities parallels what John Dewey called "the moving spirit of the whole group" (Maeroff, 1990).

TECHNOLOGY AS A TOOL FOR COLLECTING, STORING, AND ACCESSING STUDENT INFORMATION

A certain amount of record keeping is necessary for effective advisement. Achievement test scores, academic grades, and other records of academic progress and learning style profiles are basic to the advisement process. These records are usually maintained in confidential folders or dossiers housed in the student services area. As a result, they are not easily accessible to teacher-advisers. With the advent of computer technology and school networking, information contained in these records is more accessible to educators with a need to know. When advisers confer with individual advisees and/or their parents, they need to be able to access information germane to the discussion. Correspondingly, as they work closely with their advisees, they need to be able to add to the school database.

For example, in a school operating a continuous progress approach to curriculum and instruction, each student's academic progress is recorded in a central database. When teacher-advisers meet with advisees, parents, or other teachers, they can readily see the progress a student is making in each subject area. As a student completes units of work toward the successful completion of a course the information is recorded in the student's technological dossier. Thus, advisers, advisees, teachers, administrators, and parents can obtain immediate feedback on any student's progress in school. In time, the traditional report card can be replaced by a report of student progress whenever it is requested. The proliferation of personal computers in homes will allow for the possibility of daily checks by parents on their child's schoolwork.

Teacher-advisers can also assist advisees with the creation of academic resumes to attach to their transcripts. Electronic credential-building gives the adviser and the advisee the flexibility of revising the materials over the course of a student's longevity in a particular school. This process also helps students see the connection between what they do in school and the expanded reality of the world outside the school. It may just be a matter of time before all students have their own CD to record their school careers complete with multimedia accouterments. One value of the expanded student record is the more complete view that it provides of a student's accomplishments. Projects can be described fully; school and community service explained and student strengths explicated.

Advisers can record the hours an advisee spends in community service. They can also keep track of personal activities such as ballet, distance running, workouts at fitness centers, and bicycling that may be integrated with school activities to gain credit in physical education. Technology enables the school to get a comprehensive record of a student's accomplishments. This process is facilitated when teacher-advisers know how to store and access information. The traditional permanent record of student work housed in files in the guidance department is replaced by a system that provide the means for instant access and accurate communication.

The required skills and information for proper advisement can be offered in several formats. In addition to workshops, university coursework, independent reading, and one-on-one meetings with specialists, most schools with advisement programs develop a handbook to help teacher-advisers with their responsibilities. The contents of these handbooks may vary slightly from school to school and may contain different kinds of information for middle and high school levels. Chapter 7 offers suggestions for developing an advisory handbook that is a guide for teachers defining their role and responsibilities as advisers.

TACTICS

♦ The advisement apprenticeship

One effective way of helping teachers new to a school where advisement has been in operation for one or more years is to place them for a school year as an assistant to one of the school's effective teacher-advisers. In this way, the new teacher can gain an understanding of what advisement entails and work his or her way into the program gradually. As an adviser-assistant the new teacher can observe the work of a "master" adviser. When the assistant begins to assume some of the tasks of the adviser, the adviser observes and provides feedback The close working relationship between the teacher-adviser and the adviser-assistant inducts the new teacher into the culture of advisement. This approach is especially useful if staff development funds are in short supply. It is also useful for trying out some of the information and skills offered in staff development programs.

♦ Workshops or courses

When funds are available, workshops and/or university courses are probably the best alternative. Workshops in the summer months of June and/or August can provide team building and support for advisement. Helping advisers become familiar with course offerings and instructional approaches in various departments can be accomplished in a 30-hour workshop. The process not only informs teacher-advisers it can begin the building of a sense of community, a collective responsibility for student learning, and communication skills. Sixty-hour workshops can address cognitive-learning styles, choice theory, or listening skills. During the school year, university courses in any of these topics can be offered for graduate credit or credit toward recertification. Sometimes universities are willing to offer courses on a school campus. In other cases, an outside agency, such as Educator Training Center, can arrange for the credit and offer instruction. The active participation of the principal and other school leaders in either workshops or courses strengthens the faculty's commitment to improving their advisement skills. In some cases, the principal and a teacher elected by the faculty can form a team to deliver all or part of the content.

♦ Individual conferences

Individual conferences between teacher-advisers and guidance counselors on a regular basis are another effective approach to staff development. By scheduling individual conferences with advisers, counselors model one of the important adviser functions. The one-to-one setting is often less threatening to teachers and offers them an opportunity to raise questions and express concerns. Individually with advisers, counselors can assist in developing strategies for improving skills and working with problem students. They can also suggest resources beyond the school in the context of advisee needs and difficulties.

♦ Visits to other schools

Personal visits to other schools implementing successful advisement programs are enlightening. Teacher-advisers talk with other teacher-advisers about their successes and problems. These meetings may lead to an understanding that the pathway to success is often cluttered with many loose ends and unforeseen circumstances. They can also lead to new insights and new techniques for improving one's role as an adviser.

♦ Including advisement in annual evaluations

This tactic is twofold. First, specific expectations for teacher-advisers can be written into the standards used to evaluate a teacher's annual performance. When so doing, it seems wise to enlist a committee of teachers to draft the expectations for faculty approval prior to implementation. The process itself can raise the level of discourse and reinforce many of the behaviors already in place. Second, placing the expectations in the annual evaluation carries a message to teachers that the advisement role is important. But, evaluation of such an significant activity seems too important to wait until the end of a school year to accomplish. It must be ongoing. Some schools have created a simple monthly form for advisers to complete in which they report the number of individual conferences with advisees, the number of parent contacts, a description of successes, and a place to request help. Additionally, the close proximity of a counselor to a cluster of advisers contributes to ongoing assessment and evaluation.

7

GETTING STARTED

The easiest way to start an advisement program is to have it be part of a new school's program and thus integral from the outset. Because this ideal opportunity is rare except in rapidly expanding school systems, this chapter focuses on getting an advisement system in place in environments where it has not previously existed. There is considerable negative national data to indicate a need for close relationships between young people and responsible adults; one need only pick up the daily newspaper or tune to the nightly news to be reminded of the problems of schools and of adolescents. The changing influence of the family further complicates matters. The increasing number of single-parent families and families with two working parents has led to youngsters who have more and more unsupervised hours and to parents who are often too fatigued to parent. In public schools, where staff responsibilities seem to be multiplying exponentially, the initial goal is to convince staff and parents that an advisement system will augment the investment in teaching and learning.

CREATING A NEED AMONG FACULTY AND PARENTS

Faculty and parents share the same concerns about any new program: the impact on instructional time and the benefits to student success. Thus, any new initiative must ultimately address these two issues. But there are other steps to be taken first.

ASSESSING NEED

Although the school leadership group may feel strongly about instituting an advisement program, it is important to determine the extent of that feeling in the school itself and in the parent community. A needs assessment, a survey, or both are useful feedback tools that can be distributed to staff, students, and parents/guardians for the express purpose of determining the need for a program, the level of knowledge about advisement, and the interest in and potential support for an advisement program. A needs assessment begins with a clear statement of outcomes, and then employs a commercial or locally created instrument to determine the status quo in relation to the desired outcomes. A survey also can assess support and identify questions and concerns that need to be addressed in the early stages of thinking and planning.

GATHERING DATA

In today's data-driven public school environments, the school leadership team must also gather available data to demonstrate a need for action. Among the possible resources are test scores over a period of years; demographic data, such as the number of racial/ethnic groups in the student body, the number of single-parent families, the number of homes where English is not spoken; socioeconomic data, such as the number of students receiving free or reduced lunch, the number of students living in subsidized housing, the number of students needing to work to help support the family, the number of students needing financial assistance to attend college; support system data, such as available community mentor programs, connections with social agencies, support for students in the juvenile justice system. There is more data to be had than can be used purposefully, so it is important to focus on gathering only that data that relate to the specific purposes of the proposed advisement program (see Chapter 4).

BUILDING SUPPORT

This process may be long or short, but it is best that it be neither hurried nor pressured. For support to be long-standing, it must be willingly given by participants. There are multiple ways of building a support base, often termed "the critical mass." For some individuals, it is only necessary to see the needs established by a needs assessment or data to move ahead. For others, there must be opportunities for questioning, discussing, refining, and reworking. For still others, there must be an opportunity to see a viable program and to talk to *real* advisers, advisees, other staff, and parents. There are two critical factors in the support-building process: active involvement of the principal and time. The principal of the school must be committed to the undertaking. As the building leader, the principal is in a position to facilitate the development of a program and to find the resources to get a program off the ground and keep it flying. If the principal serves as an adviser, then the principal sends a message that advisement is vitally important. The issue of time is equally important. Those in charge of establishing the advisement program must take all the time necessary to create the critical human mass to support the program through the challenging steps of its beginnings. A year or more is not an unreasonable period for this step.

ADVISEMENT AND
SCHOOL IMPROVEMENT

Most advisement has been a primarily academic support system. As the national movement for academic improvement in schools has gained momentum, school improvement teams have sprung up in many districts. In their development of school improvement plans, these teams identify vehicles to implement and monitor those plans. A student advisement program is a natural vehicle for close attention to the progress of student academic improvement (see Chapter 5). In *Redesigning Schools for the New Century* (1997), Howard and Keefe take a more systemic approach, viewing advisement as one component in helping a school meets its mission, vision, assumptions, and specific outcomes for students. In either approach, advisers can make use of available student performance data and can provide daily support and encouragement to students. Advisers can turn a paper plan into a human plan.

PHASES OF IMPLEMENTATION

DESIGN OF THE PROGRAM

The leadership group of the school is responsible ultimately for the design of the program but will certainly want to include students, parents, and other interested parties in working out details. The best design is one that:

+ Responds specifically to student needs (as established by the needs assessment)

+ Specifies responsibilities and communication procedures for advisers, counselors, and administrators

+ Defines the selection/assignment process

+ Establishes a specific format and time frame for adviser-advisee contact

+ Outlines an evaluation calendar, procedures, and responsibilities

+ Describes the stages, or developmental phases, of the program

COMMUNICATION TO STUDENTS AND PARENTS

This component is extremely important as it sets the overall tone of the program, establishes its significance, and defines its parameters and expected outcomes. The overall focus is on the value of the program as an academic support system for *all* students. Some details to be communicated include how many conferences an adviser will have with an advisee, how many contacts a parent can expect and how these contacts will be made, and what the chain of communication will be when a parent contacts the school. In most advisement programs, the adviser is first in the communication chain, a logical choice because the adviser is the most knowledgeable person in the building about his or her advisees.

A public relations consultant can be most helpful in planning and implementing these very important, initial communications strategies. Selling the program effectively can make the difference in a good start and a spectacular one.

STAFF DEVELOPMENT FOR ADVISERS, COUNSELORS, ADMINISTRATORS

To begin an advisement program on a sound footing, teacher-advisers must receive pretraining in the skills important to the role, both to ensure satisfactory implementation and to reinforce their confidence in their ability to be good advisers. Critical adviser skills are listening, mediating, problem solving (including a knowledge of choice theory), action planning, and monitoring progress. Even the best of teachers will profit by refresher training in these areas. Ideally, adviser staff development continues at intervals throughout the year, which will keep advisers focused and motivated. (Chapter 6 provides a description of staff development options.)

Another essential piece of staff development is to provide advisers with descriptions of the developmental phases of the program. Given that no program springs from the planning documents full blown, what should the program look like in its first year? That is, what are the essential elements that *must* be present? Then, what will the program look like in its second year? And so forth, to the point where it is expected that all elements are fully in place. It is the job of the leadership group to translate the vision of the program into an imaginable reality for which advisers can be trained, step by step, until the vision is realized.

EXAMPLE

The following is an example of development of a teacher-adviser program aimed toward the establishment of a personalized education program.

♦ Phase One

Information giving, mostly group meetings, schedule altered to allow for adviser groups to meet to get information relative to pupil progression plan, graduation requirements, course offerings, standardized tests and careers; one- and four-year plan cards; parent contacts; student advocacy.

♦ Phase Two

Schedules altered for teachers and students to permit more individual conferring and goal setting; teacher-advisers meet individually with counselors on a regular basis; parent conferences scheduled and conducted for all students; creation of teacher-adviser handbook; some consideration of previous learning history in matching students with course offerings.

♦ Phase Three

Diagnosis of individual student learning styles; learning styles information used to place students in courses and schedules; how a student learns is communicated to teachers to help them provide more appropriate learning environments; much more contact between the teacher-advisers and the advisees' teachers.

♦ Phase Four

Flexible scheduling for students with consideration given to time-of-day preferences; teacher-advisers participate in student schedule building and schedule changing.

♦ Phase Five

The development of a personalized education plan by the teacher-adviser for each advisee; teacher-advisers build student schedules and carefully monitor student progress; every attempt is made by the school to match students with programs and proper instruction; full implementation of the DPIE model —diagnosis, prescription instruction, and evaluation (see Chapter 2).

PRELIMINARY MEETING WITH ADVISEES

A boost to the entire advisement program is an opportunity for an adviser to meet with each advisee, or with the group, before the program actually begins. This step is a good icebreaker;

it helps relieve any nervousness and provides an initial positive contact between adviser and advisees.

ONGOING EVALUATION

To ensure the viability of an advisement program, evaluation is a given. From the outset an individual or group should be identified to establish evaluation measures and to oversee the process. Such tools as surveys, focus groups, and interviews provide both formative and summative feedback about the efficacy of the program. Analysis of grades, local and state test scores, and other data can shed light on the impact of advisement on student achievement. Chapter 8 addresses this topic in detail.

RESOURCES

Resources, both material and human, are essential to effective advisement. Advisers need to have all significant demographic information about advisees, with forms to record information or track conferences and with ready-to-use activities if there are to be group meetings. (See Appendices A to D.) Regular information bulletins from the guidance office are helpful.

Equally important to effective advisement are human resources, that is, knowledge of the appropriate person to contact for various needs. A "Whom to Contact for What" list is an essential item for an adviser.

An almost invaluable resource to an advisement program is an adviser leadership group or an adviser coordinator. This group or individual (usually a teacher or counselor) provides a number of services that contribute to the smooth functioning of the program. At River Hill High School, an advisory group program committee designs advisory group time and activities; this group includes the principal, the student government adviser, a counselor, and the teacher who heads the ninth-grade team. At Wilde Lake High School an adviser coordinator works with the administration and the guidance office to provide the following services to advisers:

♦ Maintains a reasonable calendar of events (including managing the paper flow into groups)

- Coordinates the training program for advisers
- Acts as an advocate and liaison for advisory groups with the administration
- Acts as a public relations person for the advisement program
- Assists in cluster meeting planning with counselors
- Coordinates the adviser selection process and handles adviser change requests
- Participates in the ongoing evaluation of the advisory program (Advisory Task Force, 1987)

CREATING AN ADVISEMENT HANDBOOK

As an adviser program develops, it is wise to concurrently develop a handbook. As a handy reference for the experienced adviser and a lifeline to the new adviser, a handbook is simply essential to keeping everyone on the same page. The beginning handbook contains at least these items: expected outcomes, program organization, responsibilities, a yearly calendar, copies of all necessary forms, and a list of material and human resources. Over time, a handbook gains other sections, but it is important to keep the contents manageable. The primary goal of the handbook is to be useful. The following 11 topics are taken from teacher-adviser handbooks developed by schools in the Florida Teacher-as-Adviser program for high schools and a comparable middle level advisement project in the same state.

1. Overview and Organization

   This section includes a general description of the advisement program and the manner in which the program is organized. There is a delineation of the responsibilities of the teacher-adviser and the guidance counselor, along with a statement of how the two roles complement each other. There may be a list of members of the adviser leadership group.

2. The Advisement Calendar

This calendar is a month-by-month listing of the tasks to be accomplished. Usually the school year begins with a check of each student's schedule and a review of long-range goals. At the high school level, the adviser and the advisee inspect and update the Four-Year-Plan card. Parent contact is made by letter or telephone. At the middle level, a personal interview covers summer accomplishments and new directions. There may be an expectation for get-acquainted group activities. Throughout the year, activities coincide with events that affect students' academic standing, such as testing, course selection, and college applications. (Figure 7.1, pages 118–119, is a sample advisement calendar.)

3. A Guidance Scope and Sequence by Grade Level

Given the close working relationship between teacher-adviser and counselor, a logical extension of the advisement calendar is a scope and sequence of guidance activities. The scope and sequence contains key outcomes for all students by grade levels. The sixth and ninth grades might focus, for example, on adjustment to a new school environment and the academic requirements for being a successful student. Study skills, career information, interpreting tests, and building academic credentials may all be included in a scope and sequence geared to the developmental needs of students at different grade levels.

4. Personal Folders and Contents

This section describes the information to be recorded and kept individually for each advisee. Generally, the folder includes a personal data sheet, the long-range plan card, the advisee's schedule, proficiency/deficiency notices, report cards, test results, conference notes, contacts with parents, disciplinary referrals, behavior plans, and awards and other recognition received by the advisee.

FIGURE 7.1. A SAMPLE HIGH SCHOOL
ADVISEMENT YEARLY CALENDAR

- September
  - Interview each advisee; orient new advisees
  - Verify student credits
  - Ensure that each advisee's schedule is appropriate
  - Develop or update a personalized four-year plan for each advisee
  - Contact parents by telephone or mail
- October
  - Explain district testing program and state testing program
  - Conduct career survey; orient advisees to career center
  - Provide college-bound advisees with planning, testing, and financial information
  - Distribute college testing information
- November
  - Review progress reports with advisees
  - Arrange parent conferences
  - Publicize college/career information night
  - Attend adviser staff development session
- December
  - Discuss standardized testing results with individual advisees
  - Register advisees for second semester as applicable
- January
  - Review midterm examination schedule
  - Review with senior parents their student's graduation status

- Attend adviser staff development session
- ◆ February
  - Review semester progress reports with advisees
  - Arrange parent conferences as needed
  - Discuss options with non-college-bound seniors
- ◆ March
  - Review four-year plans with first-year students
  - Assist advisees in course selections based on four-year plans
  - Attend adviser staff development session
- ◆ April
  - Review progress reports with advisees
  - Arrange parent conferences with failing students
  - Conduct junior credit check; contact parents
  - Review graduation status of seniors; contact parents
- ◆ May
  - Conduct sophomore credit check; contact parents
  - Review Senior Week schedule/expectations with seniors
- ◆ June
  - Update advisee files
  - Contact parents of freshmen
  - Complete annual summary reports
  - Attend graduation, advisee family celebrations!

(Adapted from Keefe, 1983)

5. Promotion and Graduation Requirements

Most school districts have a promotion guideline
that outlines how a student advances from one
grade level to the next. A teacher-adviser must be
well versed in this information as the teacher-adviser needs to review it with advisees in discussions
of their progress.

6. Planning

A key role of advisement is helping a student prepare for the future by setting directions. High
schools often label this activity a four-year plan. At
the middle-level school, it might be called a three-
year plan. At either level, one year of the plan outlines the courses to be taken in that year. The adviser
must understand what these plans aim to do and
how they relate to one another and the advisee's
goals. Some schools even use a specific goal-setting
activity with advisees in order to reduce the dispar-
ity between student aspirations and life's realities.
Such an activity contains a series of questions about
what students wish to accomplish within a given
time frame and ideas for getting there. The adviser
and advisee complete this activity in a conference.

7. Registration and Scheduling

Because advisers are in the unique position of
knowing advisees better than any other professional in the school, they help advisees choose classes
appropriate to their aspirations and current level of
academic functioning. The adviser needs information about the content and sequence of the school
program. This information is often available
through a special publication, such as a high school
program of studies.

8. Schoolwide Testing

The adviser needs information about the tests the
school gives to assess academic achievement, learning style, attitudes, and interests, or other areas. The

handbook provides the testing schedule plus a short description of each test.

9. Interviewing Guidelines

   Teacher-advisers hold both advisee and parent conferences, so it is advisable to include guidelines for conducting them. Procedural checklists and sample questions are also helpful.

10. Miscellaneous

    This section varies greatly from school to school and level to level. It may include advisory group activities, athletic eligibility information, club information, or whatever else is significant to the school.

11. Forms

    This section has copies of all the forms that advisers use, with samples filled out as needed. (See Appendix F.)

Clearly, an advisement system represents an increase in responsibility for teachers. But it provides an invaluable benefit for students and parents. What then of the two issues raised at the beginning of the chapter—the impact on instructional time and the benefits to student success? We contend that advisory time *is* instructional time. More important, each student being known individually, each student receiving one-on-one help in learning and applying lifelong planning, study, evaluation, and interpersonal skills under the mentorship of a caring adult is an outcome that is, quite simply, priceless.

8

ASSESSING PROGRESS

Assessment is the word of the day—alternative assessment, authentic assessment, criterion-referenced assessment, formative assessment, on-demand assessment, performance assessment, preassessment, postassessment, summative assessment! Because of the vital importance of advisement and its potential impact on the lives of young people, assessment must be a part of any advisement program. Is the program meeting specific objectives? Is there progress toward overall outcomes? Is student academic performance improving? Are parents pleased? Are advisers pleased? Are students satisfied? When assessment is built into the program, there is a constant source of data to evaluate effectiveness and to direct adjustments.

MONITORING THE PROGRAM

The overall monitoring of the program is the responsibility of the school leadership group, a subgroup, or an individual that has assumed the responsibility. In the design phase, the leadership group establishes outcomes and objectives for the program. At that time, the group also identifies assessment methods, performance standards, and milestones. The task during the school year is to collect data—both print and personal —at specified times, analyze it, and decide whether to make adjustments in the program.

There are numerous kinds of data to collect and many ways to monitor the advisement process. To track the degree of communication taking place, an adviser might keep a log of conferences with advisees, meetings with individual teachers, referrals to guidance, and calls to parents. The collection of this kind of data is enhanced when advisers receive a weekly bulletin, a calendar, or a checklist that pinpoints specific information to be compiled. Requiring a report at regular intervals, monthly or quarterly, is also useful. In a new advisement program, gathering this kind of information provides *baseline data* that can be used to set future goals and against which progress toward these goals can be measured.

To monitor an adviser's conference skills, a counselor or administrator might participate in some of the individual conferences or interview advisees randomly to determine their understanding of elements such as learning style and personal plans. Advisers themselves might pair up in a peer-coaching arrangement and serve as process observers for each other in nonconfidential conferences with advisees or in group activities. Peer coaching is a proven, nonthreatening process that helps educators focus on developing specific skills and then practicing them under the knowledgeable eye of a trusted colleague. The relationship of peer coaches is not unlike the adviser-advisee relationship, the difference being that each individual in the coaching pair is sometimes adviser, sometimes advisee.

Another aspect of monitoring is regular communication among members of a cluster. In the administrator-counselor-adviser cluster, each cluster meets regularly, at least quarterly, to review data, share successes, discuss problems, and plan ahead for activities for advisees.

Still another aspect of monitoring is advisee self-monitoring. Advisees can regularly review their role in the process, using a checklist, Likert scale, or rubric. Are they getting to conferences and group meetings on time? Are they using their learning style profile to facilitate their learning in their classes? Are they using time wisely, getting homework done, meeting deadlines, juggling academics and extracurricular activities effectively? Are they relying on the adviser for advice, support, and assistance?

Historically, American education has often put programs in place and devised an evaluation system after the fact. It is significant to effective monitoring to have an evaluation system in place as the program begins so that everyone knows her or his responsibility, and when and how to collect the data that is needed at any given point.

DETERMINING
PROGRAM EFFECTIVENESS

A look at program effectiveness is both a short-term and long-term task, that is, both formative and summative. It is also a task that involves assessing not only the major purpose of advisement—academic achievement—but also other aspects of the program, such as growth in interpersonal skills and problem-solving skills. The periodic assessments during a school year—the formative assessments—are important checks for keeping adviser and advisees focused and moving forward. The end-of-year assessment and the end-of-program assessment (when the advisee graduates) are summative assessments that focus on the advisee's academic achievement and skills growth. Once again, intended outcomes frame the procedure. And benchmarks, or milestones, establish the points at which progress toward the outcomes will be measured. What might a school consider to determine effectiveness of an advisement program?

ACADEMIC ACHIEVEMENT

With academic achievement being the primary goal of advisement, regular reviews of student performance are a must. The adviser leadership group will want to set improvement targets for advisers and advisees, basing those targets on data already at hand. For example, one target may be to have a percentage of students achieve an identified grade-point average for a marking period or for the year. Or a target might be an individual improvement goal for each advisee based on performance in the previous year or performance at the end of the first marking period. Other targets might be a percentage increase in the number of students taking more demanding courses or pursuing independent research or working with mentors. Yet another target might be to have all seniors compile and present a portfolio in an area of interest or to have more students pursuing additional education beyond high school. Over time, this quantitative data provides a visual picture of academic progress, a basis of comparison from year to year, and an indicator of needed adjustments to the program.

Collecting qualitative data is also worthwhile. Questionnaires and interviews with students provide rich information that figures and charts do not. Designing a set of questions to elicit student opinions of the value of their course work and projects, their academic discussions with their advisers, or their personal plans is the first step. The interviewers may be counselors, or central office staff, or trained volunteers, including upperclass students. Although there will be considerable variety in responses, patterns will emerge and point the way for needed changes.

GROWTH IN INTERPERSONAL AND PROBLEM-SOLVING SKILLS

Feedback from business and industry indicates that a major ability needed in today's workers is the ability to work effectively with others, particularly in small groups or teams, to solve problems. This area is one whose assessment would involve a combination of quantitative and qualitative data. Student participation in advisory group problem-solving discussions, in performance assessment group work in classes, in extracurricular activities such as athletic teams and mock trial competitions, or in community service projects would provide quantitative evidence of exposure to problem-solving situations. Qualitative assessment might include reflective writing by an advisee, or an evaluation sheet from a judge, or an assessment from a sponsor.

GROWTH IN SELF-MANAGEMENT

In middle school or high school, a major goal for an advisee is to be able to review one's situation, make plans for improvement, and see those plans through. This is a skill that develops faster for some advisees than for others. The ultimate role of the adviser is precisely that—adviser—one who facilitates, not one who directs. Adviser and advisee can together set targets, gradually increasing the expectation for the advisee to be self-managing. Self-assessment by the advisee, using a checklist or rubric developed by the adviser leadership, provides one measure of the effectiveness of the advisement program.

Long-Term Benefits

The ultimate test of an advisement program is that it is viewed as valuable when the student is moving to another level and after the student has graduated. This data is particularly significant for maintaining support for advisement. A survey using Likert scales, a questionnaire, or an interview can provide useful information about the long-range benefits of advisement (see Figure 8.1). Gathering this information as a student leaves middle school for high school or leaves high school for college, vocational training, or a job provides looking-back, looking-ahead information. Gathering information a year or so after an exit adds the perspective that is gained from distance. Gathering parent data at these points is also useful. Using this data, a school improvement team or the adviser leadership can adapt an advisement program to make it more powerful. It is important to be reminded here of something that every educator knows—what gets tested gets taught. Relating this to advisement, what is established as a target will get attention.

Making Changes Based on Information

After data has been collected and analyzed and the progress toward targets and outcomes assessed, the school improvement team and the adviser leadership are ready to discuss possible program changes. It is critical to base changes on the information at hand, but it is important to understand that the information at hand does not always indicate what to do. Data, particularly data that are strongly affected by the interpersonal relationships that exist between advisers and advisees, can reveal a problem without giving any hint of a solution. There may need to be a decision to collect a different kind of data or more detailed data. There may be a decision simply to give a particular aspect of the program more time to work. There may even be a need to make an *educated guess* about what should be the next steps.

(Text continues on page 131.)

FIGURE 8.1. INITIAL SURVEY
FOR ELEVENTH GRADERS

Male ____ Female____ Previous school _____
Tech Magnet student ____ Adviser _____
Student within district _____ Siblings at school: Yes ___ No ___

Directions: **Please answer the following questions according to the scale below.**

0	1	2	3	4
not at all	a little	somewhat	a lot	extremely

To what extend do you feel:

1. Long Reach High is similar to your previous high school?   _____

2. rules and regulations are as strict as your previous high school?   _____

3. teachers are as caring as those at your previous high school?   _____

4. an advisory program will help you academically?   _____

5. study skills should be incorporated into advisory?   _____

6. college information should be distributed during advisory?   _____

7. college entrance requirements should be addressed in advisory?   _____

8. advisory should be used exclusively to complete homework?   _____

Mid-Year and End-of-Year Evaluation

Student Advisory Program Survey
How can we improve it?

Please fill out this survey to the best of your ability.

1. How satisfied are you with the current advisory program?

Circle a number, 1 being the least satisfied to 5 being the most satisfied:

      1   2   3   4   5

2. Rate the following details in the current program.

Circle a number, 1 being the least satisfied to 5 being the most satisfied:

The effectiveness of the presentation of the lessons

      1   2   3   4   5

The content of the lessons

      1   2   3   4   5

Interaction with the adviser

      1   2   3   4   5

How advisory groups are divided

      1   2   3   4   5

3. What suggestions do you have to revise the current program?

Check one or more of the items below you would like implemented, or write other suggestions in the space provided:

_____ Meet more than twice a week

_____ Increase advisory time

_____ Decrease advisory time

_____ Have guest speakers talk about jobs or other areas of interest

_____ Have college students come in and talk about the college experience

_____ Learn skills that will help in the real world (job interviews, résumés, college applications, etc.)

_____ Have competition among advisories

_____ Learn relaxation techniques

_____ Other_____

4. What would you like to gain from the advisory program?

    Rank the following choices from 1 to 8, 1 being the most important, 8 being the least important:

    _____ Interacting and making friends

    _____ How to cope with real life situations (decision-making)

    _____ Getting help with school work

    _____ Creative thinking skills

    _____ Developing strong personal qualities

    _____ Learning how to use today's technology

    _____ Learning time management and organizational skills

    _____ Learning how to communicate with others

5. How would you prefer to be grouped into advisories?

    Please rank the following choices from 1 to 6, 1 being the most preferred, 6 being the least preferred:

    _____ Randomly

    _____ By interests

    _____ Alphabetically

    _____ By grade

    _____ By student choice

    _____ Clubs

Comments:

Once the leadership has made tentative decisions about program adjustments, the discussion should extend to advisers and advisees for their reactions and suggestions. The core of advisement is ongoing communication between responsible adults and adolescents. Adolescents need to experience that good communication involves *all* the significant players and values *all* input at *all* stages of a project. For youngsters from stable home environments, this experience expands their skills in working as a member of a group toward a positive goal. For youngsters who have few adult role models in their lives, this experience with change as a healthy, growth-inducing process may be the only one of its kind in their pre-adult lives.

When decisions are confirmed and objectives adjusted, the process begins again: implementation, data collection and analysis, evaluation, new objectives.

BUILDING ADVISEMENT INTO
TEACHER EVALUATION

Building advisement into teacher evaluation is actually a second step. Building the expectation for advisement into the teacher interview process is the first step! But given that most advisement programs begin in schools with staff already in place, adding adviser performance to teacher evaluation is a must. Doing so is absolutely essential to the success of the advisement program. At Wilde Lake High School the principal used a teacher's postobservation conference after a classroom observation to discuss not only the teacher's classroom performance but also the teacher's performance as an adviser. Teachers brought adviser records to the conference as well as a record of parent contacts made and guidance referrals made. This opportunity to assess how the teacher was managing the adviser role and to discuss problems and successes emphasized the importance of advisement to the overall school program.

As stated earlier, it is a truism in America that what is tested is what is taught. Likewise, what is established as a teacher objective, for which there will be accountability, will get done. In most school districts, administrators and teachers work together to establish instructional objectives which will be assessed at the end of the school year. To enable teachers to be good advisers, the administration and the adviser must develop specific objectives in the critical areas of advisement. In a beginning program, every adviser will probably have the same set of objectives. As advisers become more experienced, objectives will vary more to address individual needs. In some ways this process mirrors the development of the personal plan by the adviser and advisee; the objectives set a direction, but they are changeable if necessary. Administrators and advisers will want to consider objectives in at least the following areas.

INTERPERSONAL SKILLS

Strengths in this area are a necessity if a person is to become an effective adviser. But the emphasis needs to be on *become*. One important set of adviser skills is one-on-one skills, such as talking to and listening to an advisee, interacting effectively with a colleague, and conferring with a parent. These skills are learnable, and there are daily opportunities to practice them. A second important set of skills is group skills. These skills often take more training and definitely more practice. Depending on the objectives of an advisement program, an adviser may need to learn the skills involved in running discussion groups, task groups, or focus groups. And there are activities, such as icebreakers, which are often group activities. Evaluation might include the completion of a specific number of interactions and groups, the keeping of a log by the adviser, or assessments of group activities by a process observer.

ORGANIZATION OF STUDENT INFORMATION

An adviser must keep student information in an orderly and confidential manner. Most advisers keep information either in folders or a notebook. In a school that is networked, information could be kept on a disk or hard drive. Evaluating this area requires assessing an adviser's method of organization for clarity, completeness, and orderliness.

MANAGEMENT OF COMMUNICATIONS

This area has some overlap into Interpersonal Skills, but focuses on different dimensions such as the actual tracking of communications, making decisions about whom to involve when problem-solving, following procedures for referrals, demonstrating effective writing skills on such items as college recommendations, and getting information to advisees as they need it. Given the vast amount of paper that goes into a teacher's mailbox, it is necessary to have procedures to manage the areas that affect advisees.

MONITORING OF STUDENT ACADEMIC PROGRESS

An adviser obviously has major responsibility here and tracks not only grades and credits but also an advisee's involvement in testing—standardized tests, college tests, and so on. In some states, students receive special recognition on their diploma for taking upper level courses; an adviser must be aware of such a possibility and monitor an advisee's work toward such a goal. The adviser must develop a schedule or format that ensures regular review of all areas relating to academic progress.

PROFESSIONAL GROWTH

It is important that an adviser be involved in ongoing staff development. Over time, with the gaining of skills, an adviser can move from being the recipient of staff development to being the staff developer. In some advisement programs, new advisers are apprenticed for a year to an experienced adviser, an arrangement that provides excellent professional growth for both individuals. It is simple to create objectives that monitor an adviser's attendance at required or recommended staff development sessions. Other objectives can require evidence of the transfer of learning into adviser duties.

AN EVALUATION TIME LINE

To reinforce the value of advisement, the evaluation time line for advisement should mirror the evaluation time line for the teacher. Advisement objectives are developed early in the year at the same time as teaching objectives. Advisement objectives are evaluated at the end of the year at the same time as teacher objectives. If teachers receive a midyear evaluation, so does advisement. If a teacher is using a portfolio for evaluation, the portfolio addresses advisement skills. If two teachers are working together as peer coaches, they address improvement in advisement as well as improvement in teaching. When a teacher meets with an administrator in a follow-up conference to an observation, a review of advisement is part of that conference. Periodic milestones can also be set to review adviser record keeping or conferences. The point is that advisement is given a significant place in teacher evaluation. And the result is that teachers *become* strong advisers.

9

THE IMPACT OF ADVISEMENT AND ADVOCACY

If the purpose of school improvement is to increase the likelihood that more students will succeed academically and find school a satisfying place, then establishing an advisement program seems a logical step. With today's accent on restructuring schools, it makes sense that concern for each individual student should be uppermost in the thinking of educators.

No longer are students willing to work for rewards only at the end of the learning journey. They are much more focused on their identities. Students want to be recognized initially for who they are, and then for what they do. The old adage—if you work hard you will receive recognition—doesn't seem to wash in today's ethos.

As school populations expand and schools become more impersonal, breaking down the bigness facilitates recognizing students for who they are. When students feel comfortable about their personal worth, they are more apt to choose to do school work. The teacher-adviser, as advocate for a finite number of students, is in the best position to help the school diagnose and accommodate student strengths and weaknesses, capitalize on interests, and adjust to individual differences.

When advisement is incorporated in a total school program, the school culture is positively affected; student achievement increases; teachers and administrators gain advocates among the students; a spirit of community is created; student needs are met more readily and knowledge about the school program is proliferated among teachers and parents.

AN ENLIGHTENED
SCHOOL CULTURE

According to Terrance Deal (1987), culture "imbues life with meaning and through symbols creates a sense of efficacy and control." A school's culture is found in its artifacts, such as "daily rituals, ceremonies and icons that are most conspicuous to the casual observer" (Stolp & Smith, 1995, p. 11). An institution's culture influences people quietly and over time can change them in profound ways.

In a school committed to advisement and advocacy, caring is one of the obvious cultural symbols. Every student has a person in the school whom he or she can seek out in time of crisis. Every student has a person in whom he or she can trust and confide. The involvement of teacher-advisers in the lives of their advisees transmits the message that *every* student is important.

When students are experiencing difficulty academically or with a particular class or teacher, the adviser is accessible and willing to listen. When students plan for their futures, the adviser has information about the student that can help set targets commensurate with student strengths and interests. When students encounter a personal or school problem, either the adviser can help directly in creating a plan to resolve the problem or can refer them to a counselor or administrator. The school culture promotes help giving.

By focusing on the individual within the advisory group, teacher-advisers gain an understanding of the concept of individual differences. Ms. Myrna Pigo, a teacher-adviser at Wilde Lake High School in Columbia, Maryland, once remarked: "Since becoming an adviser, I see the need to work with my classes differently. My classes are composed of individual students with differing needs and differing backgrounds. I can no longer teach them as if they are the same." As teacher-advisers work more closely with individual advisees, they learn from experience that traditional teaching benefits only some of the students. Learning how to accommodate individual differences becomes a necessity and not idealistic rhetoric.

HIGHER ACHIEVEMENT
FOR ALL STUDENTS

Although there are no direct data that link advisement programs with increased student achievement, there is much circumstantial evidence from which to draw such a conclusion. A five-year evaluation of the Teachers-As-Advisors program in Florida showed a clear decrease in the number of dropouts in high schools where advisement programs were instituted (Jenkins, 1992). One can infer from this finding that students were doing better academically than was true when the school did not have an advisement program.

Because advisers assume leadership for communicating salient information about advisees to teachers, one can conclude that as teachers use this information to personalize learning more students succeed. Additionally, advisers gather information about individual student learning styles that assist teachers to structure learning environments differently. Learning-style information about each advisee also helps the advisee and the adviser develop strategies for improving learning in areas where the advisee may be experiencing difficulty or for working effectively at home or on a job site.

When advisers call home to report an absence and inquire about a student's well being, they encourage students to attend school on a regular basis. In the Florida evaluation, improvements in attendance were found in over half of the 122 high schools participating in the Teachers-As-Advisors Project in 1990. Improved attendance often leads to improved academic performance. Certainly, when students do not attend school regularly, they rarely achieve to their potential. Students usually avoid school because they aren't doing well. Their avoidance of school contributes to a downward spiral of academic failure from which many students do not recover. Advisers can break this cycle of failure by staying positively involved with each advisee.

ADDITIONAL BENEFITS OF
ADVISEMENT PROGRAMS

COMMUNITY

A spirit of community is engendered when advisory groups work together on a project or join in a social activity. This spirit extends to the entire faculty when teacher-advisers see their role as helping others work more effectively with students. Faculty collegiality arises from teachers and advisers working together. Counselors and teacher-advisers join forces on behalf of individual students. When a need arises, teachers have a resource person to whom they can go to in the case of an individual student. If a student is doing poorly in mathematics, the teacher of mathematics can go to the adviser, share this information, and seek a better understanding of the student. The level of communication with parents is raised through conferences and other personal contacts. Parents begin to view themselves as genuine partners in the educational process.

PERSONAL GROWTH

Advisees learn more about themselves as they explore the results of achievement tests, learning style assessments, and interest inventories in one-on-one conferences with their advisers. Students learn how to accept responsibility for resolving their own problems, both personal and educational, by applying the strategies of choice theory. They are accepted for who they are, not what they do. As students learn to deal with their problems more successfully and learning environments are reorganized to accommodate student strengths and augment weaknesses, discipline problems are reduced.

INFORMATION

Students are more informed about graduation or promotional requirements and where they stand relative to those requirements. They also are more aware of their career goals and what it takes to reach them. Individual learning plans often result from advisers and advisees developing four-year plans. They match strengths and interests in the service of present and future goals. Teacher-advisers become more knowledgeable about the total school curriculum as well as cocurricular activities.

REVERSE ADVOCACY

That advisers are advocates for their advisees is obvious, but advisees also become advocates for their advisers. As advisees get to know their advisers, they make their worth known to the entire student body. Students often listen more intently to other students than they do adults. Their assessment of teachers contributes measurably to what other students think. In addition, an advisor has the support of 12 to 15 advisees. They offer cheer, humor, and sympathy on any given day. The adviser experiences the satisfaction of establishing significant relationships with advisees that frequently do not end when the advisees graduate or leave the school.

PARENT INVOLVEMENT

Parents learn quickly that the adviser is the primary link between home and school. They benefit because they have a teacher in the school whom they can contact when they have questions to ask or information to share about their child. Reports on student progress can be received whenever the parent wishes. Simply calling the adviser parents can get timely information on a student's progress in all areas of the curriculum. The adviser is the one person in the school who knows the student best and who has his or her finger on the student's academic pulse.

ADVISEMENT AS A COMPONENT OF THE SCHOOL AS A SYSTEM

When viewed in the context of the school as a total system, advisement is an innovation designed to help the school reach desirable goals. It is an outgrowth of the belief that says, "knowing individual students well is one assurance for being able to adjust curriculum and instruction to their needs."

Advisement creates a structure within a school in which it is acceptable for a student to talk seriously to an adult who is not a parent. The structure does not demand that the advisee have an intense relationship with the adviser, but it does ensure that there will be someone there to listen. When an adult listens to the concerns of a student, and really listens, the student gains a sense of importance. The advantage of the advisement system is that all students are considered worthy of the same benefits simply because they are students at the school. What they accomplish in response to this recognition adds reinforcement and frequently propels the student to greater accomplishments.

Regular meetings between advisers and individual advisees, whether they are discussions of TV shows and the latest films, sporting events or academic progress help establish a relationship that permits a student to discuss important issues when they occur. Trust is derived from honest communication between advisers and advisees and often develops from a variety of contacts.

Advisement does not occur in a vacuum. It requires adjustments in the school as a system in order to maximize benefits. Adding advisement to a teacher's already crowded schedule does not result in commitment to the role. Sometimes asking teacher-advisers to conduct group sessions, even when the material is provided in advance, asks them to do something that few secondary teachers feel prepared to do. They do not want to assume duties beyond the scope of their expertise. Working with students one-on-one is an area where teachers generally feel competent. Meeting with parents to discuss a student's academic progress is another area where teachers also feel competent.

It is important that teacher schedules are constructed to provide the time to do the advisement well. Teachers develop commitment and feel better about planning group activities with their advisees when time is provided in the regular school day.

WHAT DOES RESEARCH SAY ABOUT THE EFFECTIVENESS OF ADVISEMENT?

Simmons and Kiarich (1989) wrote as follows about successful advisory programs and their influence on school climate: "Students who have learned to cooperate and care about others help create a pleasant school atmosphere in which everyone feels a sense of security and belonging....The results are increased concern, trust, and better communication among the entire school community" (p. 13). MacIver and Epstein (1993) related advisement to dropout rates and reported: "With family and student background variables, regions, and grade organization statistically controlled, principals in schools with well-implemented advisory programs report that they have stronger guidance programs overall and lower expected drop-out rates" (p. 556). In a three-year longitudinal study of a Canadian advisement program, Ziegler and Mulhall (1994) found an increase in decision-making, in the sense of belonging in the school, and in teacher-student relations. Jenkins evaluated the effects of advisement programs in middle and high schools in Florida each year for five successive years (1986-1991). Two-hundred fifty-seven schools were involved—122 high schools and 135 middle schools. At the high school level, advisement appeared to have a decided impact on encouraging students to remain in school and graduate. There was also considerably more parent involvement in their child's education in high schools with advisement programs when compared with high schools without advisement programs. Middle schools tended to place less emphasis on the role of advisers in monitoring advisees' academic progress which seemed to account for the inability to establish a relationship between improved academic performance and the implementation of advisement programs. It was apparent, however, that advisers had a positive effect on developing student responsibility. Fewer disciplinary referrals were recorded in schools that had established advisement programs when compared with schools just beginning programs. The principal's support for advisement was found as critical to the success of advisement programs at both middle and high school. These evaluation reports are available from the Florida Department of Education, Division of Public Schools, Tallahassee, Florida.

A Prevailing Theme

Despite the paucity of formal research projects, numerous accounts attest to the effectiveness of advisement. It is a winning proposition for all the important stakeholders of a school. Students win by having someone who advocates their role in the educational process. Teachers win by having many advocates who carry a positive message beyond the advisory group members. The school wins by an improved climate for learning that values the individual and by improved student achievement. Parents win by becoming active participants in their student's education. Society wins by having competent graduates who know how to interact in a positive manner with adults and with students from different backgrounds. With regard to the latter, what the humorist Garrison Keillor (1996) said about school choice seems fitting: "The old idea of the public school (was) a place where you went to find out who inhabits this society other than people like you."

Much is written today about disruption in our public schools. The home-schooling movement, in part, has been stimulated by a desire to avoid what some parents perceive as an unsafe public school environment. This is not to suggest that advisement is a panacea to cure such ills. The problem is complex. It is to suggest, however, that when students have an adult friend, a confidante and a mentor, they are more likely to behave in a responsible manner, and when they do not, the fact that a teacher is in close proximity appropriate interventions can be instituted. The research on stress-induced behavior is rather clear, "friends can protect people in stress from a wide variety of physical and mental hazards" (Mahoney & Restak, 1998).

There are different ways to organize and deliver advisement. Local conditions may prescribe some arrangements and invalidate others. Programs are known by a variety of names, especially at the middle level. But regardless of location or label, one dominant theme prevails: "Advisement is getting to know a student well enough to know what is best for him or her" (Powell, Farrar, & Cohen, 1985). In the Carnegie Council on Adolescent Development's report, *Turning Points: Preparing American Youth for the 21st Century* (1990), the following observation concludes the section of advisement: "The effect of the advisory system appears to be to reduce alienation of students and to provide each...adolescent with the support of a caring adult who knows the student well. That bond can make the student's engagement and interest in learning a reality." School structures for advisement and advocacy cost little when compared with the human cost in their absence. Now, more than ever, our society needs young people who can connect with themselves and with a variety of others. McLuhan's global village has come to fruition. Certainly K-12 schooling is not the only institution concerned with youth, but for many it remains the one place where students can gain a modicum of control over their lives.

Personalized instruction begins and ends with individual learners. It is the learners interaction with the process of instruction that will ultimately make a difference in his or her success. Let us hope that the words of Alfred, Lord Tennyson penned over a century ago are still relevant, "Come my friends, 'Tis not too late to seek a newer world. Push off, and sitting well in order smite The sounding furrows, for my purpose holds To sail beyond the sunset...."

APPENDIX A

GROUP-BUILDING ACTIVITIES

ICEBREAKER ACTIVITY AND ADVISORY GROUP SCHEDULE FOR A SEPTEMBER WEEK

(Received By All Advisers in Advance)

Advisers:

Advisory group is a place where you can make a difference. Start building some cohesion and rapport within your group. The more comfortable advisees are, and the better they know each other and you, the better everyone's ability to cope with difficulties will be.

Try this simple, nonthreatening activity to let kids tell about themselves and to help the others know them better.

Ask your advisees to stand (or raise their hands) whenever they are a member of the group called out by the adviser.

♦ Group Categories: Call out as many as you can think of in each one.

- Class (senior, junior, sophomore, freshman)
- Place of birth (US: Northeast, South, Midwest, West Coast, Mountains, etc.; other countries)
- Position in family (only child, oldest, youngest, middle)
- Ancestry (European, Asian, African, Hispanic/Latino, American Indian, Jewish, etc.)
- Years lived at present residence (less than 1 to 5, 6 to 10, 11 to 15, more than 15)
- Favorite school subject
- Extracurricular activities (class leadership, drama, International Club, literary magazine, Math Team, music, National Honor Society, sports, student government, yearbook, etc.)

As you call out groups, always ask, "Is there anyone or any group I missed?" This will help everyone feel included even if you did not happen to think of that particular category.

Icebreaker activity adapted from the National Coalition-Building Institute; activity and schedule developed by Eric Ebersole, Advisory Group Coordinator, Wilde Lake High School.

ICEBREAKER ACTIVITY:
GETTING TO KNOW EACH OTHER

Part A. Each student will need a half sheet paper.

1. Have each student write her/his name at the top of the half sheet of paper.

2. Have the group pair off in any way they want. (You will need to participate if group number is uneven.)

3. Have the pairs exchange papers. Each partner should write one "group" the other person belongs to on that person's paper. You may need to suggest group categories like those used previously: race, gender, age group, ancestry, religion, etc. Have each person reclaim her/his own paper.

4. To get a second pairing, assign duplicate numbers to the advisees. For example, if there are 18 people, assign the numbers 1 to 9 to the first 9 people, and then assign 1 to 9 to the second 9 people. Then have the two 1s, the two 2s, and so forth pair off.

5. Repeat the step 3 exchange with these groups. Have each pair member reclaim her/his paper.

6. Finally, have each person write a third group on her/his own paper.

Part B. Collect the papers. Now quiz the advisees by reading the three groups on each paper to see if they can identify the person whose list is being read. Here are several formats for this quiz:

1. Each student writes the names individually. Then the adviser reads the right answers.

2. Students form groups (for example, by class) and try to pick the right names.

3. Students answer informally out loud.

Developed and prepared for advisory group use by Eric Ebersole, Advisory Group Coordinator, Wilde Lake High School.

SPIRIT (HOMECOMING)
WEEK ACTIVITY

Advisers:

Next week is Spirit Week, so I have chosen an activity to reflect this theme. There are often discussions about whether our school is spirited and whether it is important to be. Perhaps a concept or definition of spirit is needed.

Below is a list of 12 ways to show school spirit (compiled from interviews conducted around the school). Make 5 or 6 copies for your group.

In whatever way you see fit, break your group into small groups of 4 to 6. Give the groups 5 to 7 minutes to rate their top 5 in order of importance to their definition of school spirit. They should place a 1 in front of the most important, a 2 in front of the next important, and so on, through 5.

Have each group report their ratings tally. Read out the 5 with the highest totals.

If there is time or at your next meeting, you might have a discussion about the importance of school spirit now that it has been brought into clearer focus. Specifically, you could discuss the importance of doing the things that are on your group's list.

What Are the Best Ways to Show School Spirit?

_____ 1. Going to sporting events and supporting the teams.

_____ 2. Participating in sports and extracurricular activities.

_____ 3. Serving on or helping out with the student government or class government.

_____ 4. Doing community service in the name of the school.

_____ 5. Defending the school when others knock it.

_____ 6. Working hard in classes and getting good grades.

_____ 7. Going to dances, plays, concerts, and other activities.

_____ 8. Signing up for classes like drama, choir, yearbook, or journalism, all of which lead to extracurricular activity.

_____ 9. Showing respect of other people in school.

_____ 10. Wearing school colors and things with the school name on them.

_____ 11. Shouting the loudest at pep rallies.

_____ 12. Keeping the school building and grounds clean and in good condition.

Developed by Eric Ebersole, Advisory Group Coordinator, Wilde Lake High School.

HOLIDAY ACTIVITIES

Thanksgiving Activity:
Where Will We Feast?

Advisers:

If you are looking for a pre-Thanksgiving activity to do with your group, here is a suggestion. I have included maps of Maryland and of the United States. Have the members of your group mark on the appropriate map where they will be going to celebrate this holiday. There are several levels of detail at which you can do this:

1. Just have each advisee put a mark on the geographic location.
2. Have each advisee initial the geographic location.
3. Have each advisee put a number on the appropriate map, and then on a separate sheet list the number, her/his name, and whom they will be visiting.

Winter Holiday Activity

Advisers:

With the coming of the holiday season and the tradition that often surrounds it, this is a good time to share information about our cultural and ethnic backgrounds.

For the activity next week, have your advisees get into pairs or groups of three. I suggest that you direct this pairing so as to promote more mixing in your group.

Have each student share a holiday custom associated with or a holiday fact about their background or family with the other members of the group. Examples might be a unique food a celebration, certain family roles, a family tradition, clothing worn, etc.

Although advisees will probably do so naturally, suggest to them that they choose something that they particularly enjoy, are proud of, or think others will find interesting.

After about 5 minutes, bring the groups together and ask volunteers to share a partner's information with the whole group. You may want to start things off by sharing first. Encourage questions from advisees.

Developed by Eric Ebersole, Advisory Group Coordinator, Wilde Lake High School.

GROUP AWARENESS/
ESTEEM-BUILDING ACTIVITY

Who are These People?

Directions: Read each description below and write the
name(s) of the fellow advisee(s) it describes in
the space at the right. It is possible that several
or no advisee(s) may fit the description.

Who is very quiet but seems to
be trying?

_____

Who is a strong leader with
many good ideas?

_____

Who is most willing to listen to
the ideas of others?

_____

Who can best explain to those
who do not understand?

_____

Who likes to direct others?

_____

Who likes to be told what to do?

_____

Whom would you pick to see
that a job gets done?

_____

Whom would you pick to make
sure the group enjoyed itself?

_____

Advisers: There are several ways to handle this esteem-build-
ing activity.

1. If the group is in the early phase of forming, have
advisees leave their names OFF their sheet, and
simply pass the sheets around for advisees to see
how they come across.

2.   If the group is comfortably cohesive, conduct a round-robin-style sharing.

3.   If the group is a real team, have each member state her/his choice(s) and tell the fellow advisee(s) why.

Developed by Eric Ebersole, Advisory Group Coordinator, Wilde Lake High School.

APPENDIX B

ACADEMIC MONITORING

INTERIM REPORT ACTIVITY AND SCHEDULE FOR AN OCTOBER WEEK

Advisers,

As interim reports have been distributed, now is an excellent time to review your advisees' progress with them. Please use as much time as possible next week on this task.

The activity for Wednesday is provided for assistance in getting your advisees to reflect on their progress and to maintain or adjust their behaviors appropriately. On the reverse, you will find a master of a sheet for such reflection and planning. Use it for immediate conferring and/or keep it for a reference in future conferring.

Dig in,
Eric Ebersole

Schedule for 10/7 to 10/11

Monday	Senior Memoirs sheets distributed
	National Honor Society membership solicitation
	Freshmen from these advisory groups to the Career Resource Center: Anders, Aldridge, Berkton, Cahill, Davis, Hill
Tuesday	No advisory group (late opening—attendance taken in 5-minute first period. Second and third periods approximately 30 minutes each.)
Wednesday	INTERIM REPORT REFLECTION
Thursday	Questionnaire concerning diets Individual conferences
Friday	Freshmen from these advisory groups to Career Center: Kelly, Mills, Murrow, Ewell, Porter, Satterfield, Thompson, Wilkerson, Woods
	Individual conferences

Prepared by Eric Ebersole, Advisory Group Coordinator, Wilde Lake High School

INTERIM REPORT ACTIVITY

HOW WAS YOUR INTERIM REPORT?

Fill in the chart below. Get a copy of your Interim Report from your adviser if you need one.

POSITIVE COMMENTS. I was given a positive comment in:

Course	Teacher	The Comment Was About:	I Got it Because I:	Can I Maintain It?

NEGATIVE COMMENTS: I was given a negative comment in:

Course	Teacher	The Comment Was About:	I Got it Because I:	To not get it again, I:

Developed by Eric Ebersole, Advisory Coordinator, Wilde Lake High School

REPORT CARD ACTIVITY
FOR THIRD QUARTER:

HOW I FEEL ABOUT THE THIRD MARKING PERIOD

1. The first thing I feel about my third quarter report card is
   _____.

2. I did better in _____ than my other
   classes because _____.

3. I did worse in _____ than my other
   classes because _____.

4. I learned the most when I _____.

5. I learned the least when I _____.

LAST QUARTER (Check the appropriate columns.)

	Too much	Enough	Not Enough
I studied			

	Yes	No
I did my best		
My parents think I did my best		
My teachers think I did my best		

	Too much	Enough	Not Enough
I socialized			
My parents think I worked			
My parents think I socialized			
My teachers think I worked			

There is a possibility that I will not earn credit in these courses:

COURSE   OUTLOOK (Check one)   WHAT CAN I DO?

            Fair   Poor   Bleak

Prepared by Eric Ebersole, Advisory Group Coordinator, Wilde Lake High School

CAREER ACTIVITY

How a 10th Grader Prepares
for Life after High School

Objective: To develop awareness for 10th graders of life in
the "real world"
Materials: Advisee folders
Time Allotted: One advisory period
Procedure:

Review the first page of the advisee folder. Ask if any advisees are planning to take the PSAT in October. Give them the date of the PSAT and encourage them to take it. Remind advisees that the test is given only once a year.

If advisees have NOT met with their counselor, you may need to review the video "Orientation to Guidance." **It is important that all advisees know their counselor.** Encourage them to make an appointment and not to wait until a problem arises. They will work closely with this person for the next three years.

Concentrate on the **Preemployment Experiences** (see form in Appendix F). If students have not already checked this list, ask them to do so at this time. Some items on the list will not be checked until a later time; however, if any students have interviewed a worker, or shadowed a worker, these experiences could be shared with the group. Good discussion questions include:

1. Why is it important to interview and/or shadow a worker in the field in which you are interested? (Discuss **expectations** and **realities** of jobs and careers).

2. How can one get more information about a specific job? The military? A career in designing? etc.

3. What can one learn from **volunteering** that will help one have a more honest picture of the real world?

4. Is it realistic to expect to graduate with a high school diploma and make "big money"? What if one does NOT finish high school? Discuss pros and cons of the GED vs. the HIGH SCHOOL DIPLOMA.

Closure: Follow-up can be done in future advisory meetings. Monitor advisees keeping their folders up-to-date.

Developed by Linda Lowry, Advisory Group Coordinator, Long Reach High School

APPENDIX C

PERSONAL GROWTH ACTIVITIES

TIME MANAGEMENT ACTIVITY

Advisers,

Next week's activity will be done on Wednesday and will involve a look at how our advisees are using their time. Below you will find a master of a 24-hour clock to use for this activity; put two of these on a sheet for each advisee.

1. First, have your advisees use the top clock and divide it with pie-shaped wedges to show the activities for a "model" school day—sleeping, studying, attending class, relaxing, etc.

2. Then have them divide the second clock for the actual previous day.

3. Use a comparison of the two clocks for some reflection:

    •   Have advisees do the comparison in pairs and think of ways to rectify discrepancies, *or*

    •   Have each advisee work individually to list reasons for the discrepancies and to make a plan to make normal days more like the model.

4. Collect the clock sheets and file them in advisee folders to use for conferences.

Developed by Eric Ebersole, Advisory Group Coordinator, Wilde Lake High School.

SELF-ASSESSMENT ACTIVITY

Advisers,

This week's activity continues the thread of self-assessment started with the New Year's resolutions of last week. Have advisees fill out the activity sheet individually or in pairs; if you use pairs, have advisee's exchange sheets and dictate answers to each other. Circulate as they work and use their answers to begin pertinent discussions.

IMPROVING ON ME!

Directions: On this sheet write down three words that you would like for people to think of when they think of you. Then write down some of the things you will have to do to become more like the person described by each word you have listed. Be as clear as you can. Think about what you can do today that will help you become what you want to be.

THREE WORDS   1. _____

THAT I WISH   2. _____

DESCRIBED ME.   3. _____

Things I must do starting today:

1. _____

2. _____

3. _____

4. _____

5. _____

Developed by Eric Ebersole, Advisory Group Coordinator, Wilde Lake High School.

PERSONAL INTEGRITY ACTIVITY

Advisers,

Next Friday night many of our students will be attending the Prom or some similar event. We will be having a related assembly next week, and it would be a good idea to do an activity in advisory group as well.

Below are some discussion questions relating to Prom-night activities. For those not attending the Prom, say that Prom night is a good example night on which to focus. This kind of focus is good for any night out, so encourage your advisees to participate seriously.

1. First break your group into small groups, and have them list the activities in which they will participate on Friday night.

2. Then have them review the questions for each activity on the list.

PLAYING IT SMART

1. Is it safe?

2. Do you have your parents' permission?

3. Will you know who will be there?

4. Will you know who will be driving?

5. Will you be able to arrange alternative transportation if necessary?

6. Is this activity your choice or someone else's?

Developed by Eric Ebersole, Advisory Group Coordinator, Wilde Lake High School.

APPENDIX D

SCHOOLWIDE PROBLEM-SOLVING ACTIVITIES

PROBLEM-SOLVING ACTIVITY
—BROAD FOCUS

THEME: Diversity and Human Relationships

Video: "Shadow of Hate"

Advisers: This video deals with prejudice, hate crimes, etc. The video will air on the school channel during Tuesday's advisory group. On Thursday there will be a follow-up discussion in each advisory group. Use the questions below as a guide. Please feel free to improvise and adapt the questions as needed. If you think your group will be especially challenging, ask a counselor to help you conduct the discussion.

1. What kinds of issues and attitudes cause religious intolerance?

2. What underlying economic and social factors contributed to the Irish vs. Protestant conflict in Philadelphia?

3. What are some issues of public controversy in our country today that pit one religious group against another? Discuss nonviolent ways of resolving these disputes.

4. Many of those who took part in the anti-Chinese violence were recent immigrants themselves (from the British Isles). Why do you think they considered themselves "American" and the Chinese "foreign"?

5. How does segregation contribute to intolerance? Does segregation necessarily lead to intolerance?

6. Why do we often look for scapegoats when something goes wrong? How does prejudice contribute to scapegoating?

7. Have you ever gone along with a group even though you knew what they were doing was wrong? What causes people to do this?

8. According to FBI statistics, gay people are among the most frequent victims of hate crimes. How do hate crimes against homosexuals compare with crimes against other minorities? How do you think stereotyping contributes to intolerance and violence towards gays and lesbians?

9. Why do you think strained relationships exist between two minority groups who have both experienced the pain of discrimination?

   Developed by Linda Lowry, Advisory Group Coordinator, Long Reach High School.

PROBLEM-SOLVING ACTIVITY
—SPECIFIC FOCUS

Advisers,

About a week and a half ago, a disturbing sequence of violent acts took place here culminating in the serious injury of one of our students. Throughout the development of these events, there were students present whose behavior did not help prevent or control these events and, in some cases, the student behavior even contributed to make these events worse.

As the faculty portion of the school community, we are very aware of our responsibility to help maintain a positive and safe atmosphere here. It seems that some of our students need help in defining their equally significant role in contributing to this atmosphere. It is critical for our student body to understand that their attitudes and actions, in concert with ours, have a significant impact on the quality of life in this school building.

Next week, in advisory group, we will have an activity that will involve a discussion with our advisees about these responsibilities. The administration has designated this activity as a mandatory one. Below are discussion questions to help you and your group focus. You might use all or part of the first two paragraphs above as a guide to introduce this activity.

1. Does the fact that there was physical violence in our school worry or disturb you? Why or why not?

2. Why do you think these violent acts occurred?

3. Do you feel as if you might be in personal danger at the school now or in the future?

4. How do you think this and other types of violence and intimidation affect our learning atmosphere?

5. What do you think can be done to keep negative acts like these from happening?

6. If you are present when a situation develops that disrupts the school and/or is potentially dangerous, what should your role be? In what ways can you help?

7. Why is it important to make sure that perpetrators of violent or intimidating acts are identified? When you have information about an incident, what could prevent you from sharing that information with someone who can act on it? How can you deal with threats about giving information?

> * The administration feels that these last two groups of questions come to the heart of the matter. Be certain to address them with your group. Please feed back to the administration any important information that comes out of this discussion.

> *Developed by Eric Ebersole, Advisory Group Coordinator, Wilde Lake High School.*

NATIONAL EVENT DISCUSSION ACTIVITY

January 8, 1991

Advisers,

Soon it will be January 15, and the potential for violent conflict in the Middle East looms large. Our students are young enough to have never lived during such a traumatic thing as war. The administration has asked me to design a discussion activity to explore some of the realities and feelings that exist during armed conflict. Discussion questions on a subject as significant as this one need to be chosen carefully. I am consulting written resources and our social studies teachers to help me. Information and questions will be in your boxes shortly so that you can be prepared for the discussion. This activity is mandatory.

Introduction to Advisees

Next Tuesday is the 15th of January. This is the date after which the United Nations has approved the use of force to resolve the conflict that exists currently in the Persian Gulf. United States soldiers represent the majority of the troops assembled in Saudi Arabia for this purpose. On Wednesday representatives from Iraq and the United States met and publicly expressed doubt that they had accomplished anything that might avoid armed conflict. A look at the ramifications of armed conflict is important for us all at this time.

1. How would a war in the Persian Gulf affect you?
2. Why is the United States involved in the military build-up in Saudi Arabia? What has the U.S. done up to this point to try and resolve the conflict?
3. Do you know anyone who is currently stationed in Saudi Arabia? How does that person feel about the potential war, and how do you feel about that person being there?
4. Try to imagine someone who graduated from Wilde Lake last year serving and risking her or his life in armed conflict. What emotions does this possibility stir up? Do you feel any

different knowing that women are also serving and may also die?

5. Would you sign up to help out and risk your life in this conflict? Why or why not?

6. Do you think Iraq will use chemical and/or biological weapons? What should our response be if they do?

7. Should the use of nuclear weapons be considered? Why or why not?

8. Casualty estimates have run in the hundreds of thousands. Do you think, if armed conflict begins, that it will be long lasting with many deaths, or short with few deaths? Could this war spread to become a larger conflict involving more nations?

9. Do you think that armed conflict will begin in the Middle East, or do you believe some other solution is possible? What do you see as an alternate solution?

   (This discussion yielded critical information about students who had parents, relatives, or friends who were serving in the Persian Gulf. As a result, the Guidance Department established a support group for affected students.)

   Developed by Eric Ebersole, Advisory Group Coordinator, Wilde Lake High School.

APPENDIX E

ADVISORY GROUP SCHEDULES

TRADITIONAL SIX-PERIOD SCHEDULE:
WILDE LAKE HIGH SCHOOL, 1998

	Monday-Thursday		*Tuesday-Wednesday-Friday*
First Period	7:30–8:25		7:30–8:20
		Advisory Period	8:25–8:45
Second Period	8:30–9:25		8:50–9:40
Third Period	9:30–10:25		9:45–10:35
Fourth Period (includes 3 lunches)	10:30–12:00		10:40–12:10
Fifth Period	12:05–1:00		12:15–1:05
Sixth Period	1:05–2:00		1:10–2:00

Note: As part of the six- or seven period-day model schedule, a longer advisory period is typically provided weekly or biweekly. The longer advisory period is used for group-related activities.

FOUR-PERIOD BLOCK SCHEDULE:
RIVER HILL HIGH SCHOOL, 1998

Monday-Wednesday-Friday		*Tuesday-Thursday*
First Period	7:30–8:55	7:30–8:44
Advisory Period		8:54–9:18
Second Period	9:05–10:30	9:23–10:32
Third Period (includes 4 lunches)	10:30–12:30	10:37–12:36
Fourth Period	12:35–2:00	12:41–2:00

SAMPLE SCHEDULE FROM THE COALITION OF ESSENTIAL SCHOOLS

Time	Monday	Tuesday	Wednesday	Thursday	Friday
7:00	Band, choir, other activities				
8:00 Period 1	Math-Science				This is a 4-day rota- tional
	History-Philosophy				
	Arts	Generalist	Generalist	Generalist	
9:55 Period 2	Math-Science				
	History-Philosophy				
	Generalist	Arts	Generalist	Generalist	
11:45 Periods 3, 4, 5	Lunch				
	ADVISORY				
	Tutorial				
	History-Philosophy	Math-Science	Math-Science	Math-Science/ Arts	
	Arts/ Generalist	Arts/ Generalist	History-Philosophy/ Generalist	History-Philosophy	
1:45 Period 6	Math-Science				
	Arts	History-Philosophy	History-Philosophy	Arts	
	Generalist	Generalist	Arts	Generalist	
3:30	Team Meeting for Staff				
4:00– 6:00	Band, choir and other activities				

Note: Advisory is scheduled everyday and can be short-ened, extended or combined with lunch and tutorials to al-low for individual conferences and group activities.

See Sizer, 1992, p. 226.

CONTINUOUS PROGRESS SCHEDULING

(as practiced at Thomas Haney Secondary Centre)

Time	Course	Location
8:30	*Adviser Group Meeting* (Students meet with their advisers each morning to build their daily schedules, discuss problems, check progress, etc.)	
9:00		
9:30		
10:00		
10:30		
11:00		
11:30		
12:15		
1:10	*Adviser Group Meeting* (Students meet with their advisers after lunch each day for attendance check.)	
1:15		
2:00		
2:30		
3:00		

Note: The advisee and his/her adviser fill in the blanks beside each time frame other than advisory group. Most of the academic courses are offered on a continuous progress basis. Students work Independently or in learning teams completing learning guides. Some group meetings are scheduled as part of the learning guides or when necessary for course progress (e.g., choir, band).

SHOREHAM-WADING RIVER
MIDDLE SCHOOL

Period	Time	1st Quarter	2nd Quarter	3rd Quarter	4th Quarter
I.	7:50–8:30 8:30–8:42	(Music Rehearsal) ADVISORY CONFERENCE Tuesday, Wednesday, Thursday ADVISORY GROUP MEETING			
II.	8:44–9:24	Academic	Physical Ed.	Academic	Physical Ed
III.	9:26–10:06	Math	Math	Math	Math
IV.	10:08–10:48	Physical Ed.	Academic	Physical Ed.	Academic
V.	10:50–11:30	FOREIGN LANGUAGE (ODD DAYS) ART (EVEN DAYS)			
VI.	11:30–12:00 12:00–12:15	LUNCH ACTIVITY ADVISORY GROUP LUNCH (Advisers eat lunch with their groups)			
VII.	12:16–12:56	Reading	Academic	Reading	Academic
VIII.	12:58–1:38	Academic	Academic	Academic	Academic
IX.	1:40–2:20	Academic	Reading	Academic	Reading
	2:20–4:30	INTERSCHOLASTIC SPORTS			

MUSIC REHEARSAL SCHEDULE:

7:50–8:42 **Monday**—Orchestra Sections/Advance Band
Tuesday—Full Orchestra/Advance Band
Wednesday—Advance Band (Full)/Chorus
Thursday—Orchestra/Advance Band (Full)
Friday—Chorus (Full)

2:20–3:30 **Monday** and **Wednesday**—Intermediate Band

APPENDIX F

FORMS

ADVISEE PERSONAL DATA SHEET

Year of Graduation _____

1. Full name _____

2. Address _____ Telephone _____

   _____   _____

3. Parent/guardian occupation _____

4. Location of parent/guardian employment _____

   _____

5. Emergency contact number(s) _____

6. Previous adviser(s) _____

7. Other schools attended _____

8. Do you work after school? _____ Where? _____
   Hours _____

9. Favorite school subject(s) _____

10. Least favorite school subject(s) _____

11. Career aspirations _____
    Preparation to date _____

12. Do you plan to pursue education beyond high school? (e.g.,
    college, university, community college, junior college, tech-
    nical school, armed services, etc.) _____ Steps toward ap-
    plication _____

13. What steps have you taken toward college admission? Have
    you taken the PSAT, SAT? _____ If not, have you made
    application to take one or both? _____ What college
    campuses have you visited? _____

14. What are your major interests? _____
    What extracurricular activities do you pursue to tap these
    interests?

15. What help can I give to enable you to deal more successfully
    with school or with career aspirations?

ADVISEE ACTIVITIES SHEET

This sheet should be updated yearly. It provides a focus for advisee conferences and is a ready source of data when it is time to write recommendations for seniors.

1. Student leadership

2. Clubs or service organizations

3. Athletic teams

4. Other teams (e.g., Math Team, It's Academic Team, Debate Team)

5. Fine arts participation

6. Special projects or special services for the school

7. Special projects or special services for the community

8. Honors organizations

9. Awards and honors

CONFERENCE FORM

Advisee name _____

Telephone _____ Best time to reach parent _____

Date _____

Academic progress _____

_____

Advisee concerns _____

_____

Adviser concerns _____

_____

Action plan _____

_____

Checkpoints _____

_____

Date _____

Academic progress _____

_____

Advisee concerns _____

_____

Adviser concerns _____

_____

Action plan _____

_____

Checkpoints _____

_____

TESTS AND OTHER EXPERIENCE

Standardized Tests

I have taken:

___ PSAT/NMSQT in Grades ___   ___ SAT II in Grades _____

___ ACT PLAN in Grades _____   ___ AP in Grades _____

___ SAT I in Grades _____   ___ TOEFL in Grades _____

___ ACT in Grades _____   ___ _____ in Grades ____

Pre-Employment Experiences

Please check those you have experienced.
___ Met with guidance counselor
___ Volunteered
___ Talked with parents/adults about career plans
___ Took a field trip related to a career
___ Participated in extracurricular activities
___ Wrote for information on careers
___ Explored occupations in Career Center
___ Took part in a career day
___ Computer-based resources
    ___ VISIONS   ___ BEACON
    ___ GIS   ___ Other
___ Held part-time or summer jobs
___ Heard speakers or college reps
___ Interviewed a worker
___ Completed leadership training or held office
___ Observed (shadowed) a worker
___ Attended a college fair
___ Completed a résumé
___ Interviewed with a college
___ Job interview
___ Filled out applications

Work Experience
(Include volunteer and part-time work)

Employer	Date	Type of Work	Skills Acquired	The Most Important Thing I Learned

REFERENCES

Abbott, J. (1997). To be intelligent. *Educational Leadership, 54*(6), 6–10.

Advisory Task Force (1987). *Report to the faculty.* Columbia, MD: Wilde Lake High School.

Carnegie Council on Adolescent Development's Task Force on Education for Young Adolescents (1990). *Turning points: Preparing America's youth for the 21ˢᵗ century.* Waldorf, MD: Carnegie Council on Adolescent Development.

Clerk, F.E. (1928). *A description and outline of the operation of the adviser-personnel plan at New Trier High School.* Winnetka, IL: New Trier High School.

Cushman, K. (1990, September). Are advisory groups "essential"? What they do, how they work. *Horace, 7,* 1.

Deal, T. E. (1987). The Culture of Schools. In *Examining the Elusive. The 1987 ASCD Yearbook.* Alexandria, VA: Association for Supervision and Curriculum Development.

Edwards, J. (1991, January). To teach responsibility, bring back the Dalton plan. *Phi Delta Kappan,* 398–401.

Elam, S.M., Rose, L.C., & Gallup A.M. (1997, September). The 29th Annual Phi Delta Kappa/Gallup poll of the public's attitude toward the public schools. *Phi Delta Kappan, 79,* 1.

Florida Department of Education (1990). *Florida's middle school advisement program.* Tallahassee, FL: Division of Public Schools, Bureau of Support Services, Student Services Section.

Florida Department of Education (1991). *Florida's middle school advisement program.* Tallahassee, FL: Division of Public Schools, Bureau of Support Services, Student Services Section.

Florida Department of Education (1986). *Teachers-as-advisors program*. Tallahassee, FL: Division of Public Schools, Bureau of Support Services, Students Services Section.

Florida Department of Education (1987). *Teachers-as-advisors program*. Tallahassee, FL: Division of Public Schools, Bureau of Support Services, Students Services Section.

Florida Department of Education (1988). *Teachers-as-advisors program*. Tallahassee, FL: Division of Public Schools, Bureau of Support Services, Students Services Section.

Florida Department of Education (1989). *Teachers-as-advisors program*. Tallahassee, FL: Division of Public Schools, Bureau of Support Services, Students Services Section.

Florida Department of Education (1990). *Teachers-as-advisors program*. Tallahassee, FL: Division of Public Schools, Bureau of Support Services, Students Services Section.

Florida Department of Education (1991). *Teachers-as-advisors program*. Tallahassee, FL: Division of Public Schools, Bureau of Support Services, Students Services Section.

Gardner, H. (1983). *Frames of mind: The theory of multiple intelligences*. New York: Basic Books.

Glasser, W. (1972). *The identity society*. New York: Harper & Row.

Glasser, W. (1986). *Control theory in the classroom*. New York: Harper & Row.

Glasser, W. (1990). *The quality school: Managing students without coercion*. New York: Harper Perennial.

Glasser, W. (1998). *Choice theory: A new psychology of personal freedom*.

Jenkins, J.M. (1997, April). Advisement and advocacy: Personalizing the educational experience. *NASSP Practitioner, 23*(4).

Jenkins, J.M. (1996). *Transforming high schools: A constructivist agenda*. Lancaster, PA: Technomic Publishing.

Jenkins, J.M. (1992). *Advisement programs: A new look at an old practice*. Reston, VA: National Association of Secondary School Principals.

Jenkins, J.M. (1992, January). Personalization education through advisement. *International Journal of Educational Reform, 1*(1), 73–75.

Keefe, J.W. (1983, June). Advisement—A helping role. *NASSP Practitioner, 9*(4),

Keefe, J.W., & Ferrell, B.G. (1990, October). Developing a defensible learning style paradigm. *Educational Leadership,*

Keefe, J.W., & Jenkins, J.M. (1997). *Instruction and the learning environment.* Larchmont, NY: Eye on Education.

Keefe, J.W., & Howard, E.R. (1997). *Redesigning schools for the new century: A systems approach.* Reston, VA: National Association of Secondary School Principals.

Keillor, G. (1996, September 29). The future of nostalgia. *New York Times Magazine,* 68.

Letteri, C. (1980, March/April). Cognitive profile: Basic determinant of academic achievement. *Journal of Educational Research, 734,* 195–199.

Lowery, R. (1977, November). Bishop Carroll High School. *NASSP Bulletin, 61,* 412.

Mac Iver, D., & Epstein, J. (1991). Middle grades research: Not yet mature but no longer a child. *Elementary School Journal, 93*(5), 519–533.

Maeroff, G.I. (1990). Getting to now a good middle school: Shoreham-Wading River. *Phi Delta Kappan, 71*(7), 505–511.

Maerhoff, G.I. (1986, June). Let's hear it for New Trier. *Town and Country,* 144–147, 176, 182.

McPartland, J., Jordan, W., Legters, N., & Balfanz, R. (1997). Finding safety in numbers. *Educational Leadership, 55*(2), 14–17.

Mahoney, D., & Restak, R., M.D. (1998). *The longevity strategy.* New York: John Wiley & Sons.

Meier, D. (1996). The benefits of smallness. *Educational Leadership, 54*(1), 12–15.

National Association of Secondary School Principals (1996). *Breaking ranks: Changing an American institution.* Reston, VA: National Association of Secondary School Principals.

New Trier Township High School (1990-91). *Student guide book.* Winnetka, IL: New Trier Township High School.

Powell, A.G., Farrar, E., & Cohen, D.K. (1985). *The shopping mall high school.* Boston: Hougthton Mifflin.

Rasmussen, K. (1998). Looping: Discovering the benefits of multiyear teaching. *Education Update, 40*(2), 1, 3–4.

Raywid, M.A. (1998). Small schools: A reform that works. *Educational Leadership, 55*(4), 34–39.

Rivera-Lyles, J. (1998, October 16). White House praises Dade school. *Miami Herald,*

Shoreham-Wading River Middle School. One on one: A middle school advisory system. *Middle School Friday Memo.*

Simel, D. (1998). Education for *Bildung*: Teacher attitudes toward looping. *International Journal of Educational Reform, 7*(4), 330–337.

Simmons, L., & Klarich, J. (1989). The advisory curriculum: Why and how. *NELMS Journal, 2*(2), 12–13.

Sizer, T. R. (1992). *Horace's School.* Boston: Houghton-Mifflin.

Stolp, S., & Smith, S.C. (1995). *Transforming school culture: Stories, values, and the leader's role.* Eugene, OR: Educational Resources Information Center, Clearinghouse on Educational Management.

Viadero, D. (1996, June 12). Environmental Studies. *Education Week,* 35–38.

Ziegler, S., & Mulhall, L. (1994). Establishing and evaluating a successful advisory program in a middle school. *Middle School Journal, 25*(4), 42–46.